The
Yachtsman's
A to Z

The Yachtsman's A to Z

HENRY CLARKSON

DAVID & CHARLES
Newton Abbot London

British Library Cataloguing in Publication Data

Clarkson, Henry
 The yachtsman's A to Z
 1. Yachts and yachting—Dictionaries
 I. Title
 797.1'24'03   GV813

 ISBN 0–7153–7561–X

Photoset and printed in Great Britain
by Redwood Burn, Trowbridge & Esher.
for David & Charles (Publishers) Limited
Brunel House Newton Abbot Devon

INTRODUCTION

My intention in this concise encyclopedia is to help the young and less experienced sailor to identify by illustration terms and objects dealing with seamanship, boats and the sea. No book of this kind can cover every aspect comprehensively but I have at least made every effort to keep abreast with the latest inventions and methods. Older items and terms have been included when they seem still to have significance or interest. This is a reference book with no pretensions to being a textbook and when a drawing gives an adequate explanation in itself the text has been kept correspondingly brief.

I wish to acknowledge my gratitude to the many people who have helped me including club officials, boat builders and the yachting fraternity in general, not least Mr Royston Raymond who went through the text with a toothcomb, checking and modifying it as necessary.

Henry Clarkson
September 1978

A

Aback

Of a square sail pressed back against the mast by the wind. Sails are sometimes 'laid aback' intentionally to deaden the way.

Wind on the weather instead of the leeward side.

Abaft

Behind or towards the stern of a vessel. The word is only relative to objects and not to be confused with 'aft'.

Abeam

At right angles to fore and aft line of vessel.

A'board

On board; into or within a ship or boat.

Admiral's Cup

A cup presented to the winners of the RORC (Royal Ocean Racing Club) series of races.

Admiralty (British)

The governing authority for administration of British naval affairs. Also issues information regarding the Lists of Lights, Charts, Pilot Books, Signals, Tide Tables, etc.

Adrift

(1) Anything that has broken away from a ship, or a boat cut loose from her moorings; at the mercy of the tide. (2) A term sailors use when late.

'A' Bracket

A two-arm rigid strut constructed externally to carry the propeller shaft.

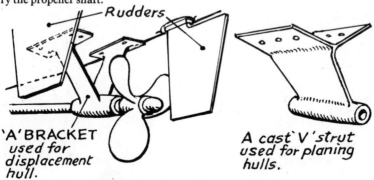

Rudders

'A' BRACKET used for displacement hull.

A cast 'V' strut used for planing hulls.

Advance

The distance made by a vessel in the line of a previous course after the helm has been applied, as for a tack: if the vessel changes her course at C and moves in a curve to A, the advance is AB.

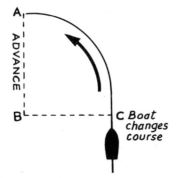

Adze

A boatbuilding tool with the blade set at right angles to the handle for chipping or slicing away the surface of the wood.

Aerofoil

The curved cross-section of a sail viewed from above on which the wind acts, like the aerofoil wing of an aeroplane, or a bird's wing.

Aft

Behind, towards the after or stern part of a vessel, as, towing a boat 'aft'.

Afterpart

That part of a vessel abaft the beam or nearest the stern.

Agonic Lines

Lines of no magnetic variation. The variation of the compass is different at different places; where the magnetic meridian coincides with the true meridian the variation is said to be *zero*, and lines connecting these are called agonic lines.

━━━━ No Variation
──── Westerly Variation
- - - - Easterly Variation

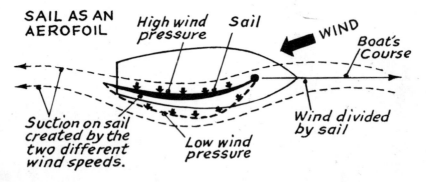

SAIL AS AN AEROFOIL

Aldis Lamp
A portable, electric-flash, signalling lamp (invented by A. C. W. Aldis); useful in boats.

Almanac
The nautical calendar, or year book, containing astronomical calculations, and other information useful to mariners.

Aloft
Anywhere above the vessel's deck.

America's Cup
A race in which the larger class of yachts take part, such as the 70ft long, 12 metre class yacht. The trophy was won by the yacht *America* from the British in 1851.

Amidships
The middle portion of a ship. The intersection of two lines, one drawn from stem to stern, the other across the beam.

Amplitude
In nautical astronomy, the amplitude of a celestial body is its angular distance from the east or west point of the horizon when the body is rising or setting. Using the sun, if E represents the true east point, S the sun and O the observer, the angle EOS is the amplitude.

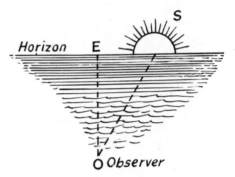

Anchor
To attach any floating object to the sea-bed. There are various types of anchor for different purposes. Shown are parts of the anchor and a few examples.

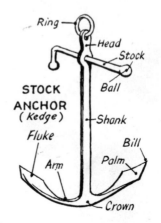

9

Danforth

Sand Anchor

Plough Type

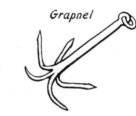
Grapnel

CQR Anchor

Stockless

Anchoring a Boat

A seaman *lowers* the anchor never throws it. When the anchor is holding, take a transit of two objects on shore and periodically make sure they are still in line. If they separate your anchor is dragging. A few tips: when anchoring always make sure end of warp is secured inboard. Always check depth of water and type of sea-bed. Keep well clear of obstructions to prevent damage. Approach anchorage heading into the wind.

Anemometer

An instrument devised by Dr Robinson for measuring the force of wind velocity.

Aneroid

A barometer, the action of which depends on the varying pressure of the atmosphere upon the depressible top of a metallic box from which the air has been exhausted. An index shows the variation of pressure. Mostly used by yachtsmen.

Angle of Outboard Motor

For efficient use of the motor, the propeller must be so angled as to push, and not lift or drag the hull. An incorrectly angled drive can cause a great loss of power.

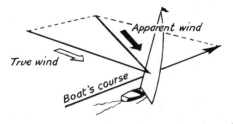

Apron

(or Stemson). A backing or strengthening timber fastened to the stempost of a vessel.

Angular Distance

The angle formed by the lines drawn from the eye to objects A and B as shown in the diagram.

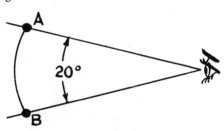

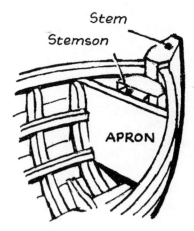

Anti-Fouling

A specially prepared paint used for coating the bottom of a boat to kill or prevent marine growth, or borer.

Apparent Wind

There are two winds—true and apparent. The true wind is when a boat has stopped and the burgee indicates the direction of the wind. The apparent wind is the deflected wind that results from the boat moving against (or across) the true wind. When sailing, the sails must be trimmed in relation to the apparent wind, not the true wind.

Archboard

The shaped piece of timber which forms the after end of a counter-stern, level with the deck.

Artificial Respiration

Resuscitation of an apparently drowned person. One of several methods is shown, the mouth–to–mouth method, which is by far the best. (Take deep breath, seal your lips round the casualty's open mouth keeping his nostrils closed all the time with your thumb and forefinger. Then blow until you see his chest rise. Repeat until he starts breathing naturally.) Others are: Holger-Nielsen method, the well known method of back

11

pressure, arm lift. Sylvester-Brosch method, the more effective manual method of chest pressure, arm lift.

Aspect Ratio

The comparison between the height of a sail and its width at the foot; a tall narrow sail has a high aspect and vice versa. Also applies to any other object, such as a rudder or centreboard.

Astern

At any point behind; away from the vessel in the direction opposite to her course; or going backward.

Athwartships

(Position). Across the boat from side to side: comparing the relative positions of objects which lie inboard on the same side of the deck.

Automatic Direction Finder

Gives instantaneous bearings of the transmission station(s).

Automatic Pilot

A convenient device for eliminating the effort of steering. It steers the vessel automatically when set on any desired course.

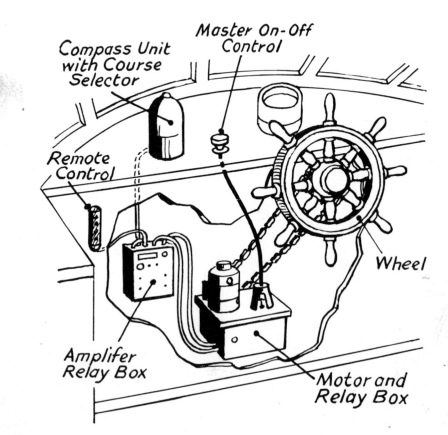

Auxiliary Engine

In some small offshore cruisers it is useful as a second string in case of calms or contrary tides. Whether the engine is inboard or outboard depends on the type of boat.

Avast

Stop. Cease. 'Avast heaving' means 'Stop hauling on that rope'.

A'weather

Towards the wind, said of a sail when it is sheeted to windward.

Azimuth

The angle or arc of the horizon that a vertical plane passing through a heavenly body makes with the meridian of the place of observation. Thus, if NESW represents the visible horizon N the north point, S the south point—the sun and C a point vertically below the sun, the arc NC of the horizon intercepted between N and C is the azimuth of the sun.

Azimuth Compass

(or Circle). An instrument containing a mirror and prism which fits on to the standard magnetic compass. It is used for taking bearings of both terrestrial and celestial objects. The circle is graduated in degrees, and these are subdivided into divisions of 15, 20, or 30 minutes each.

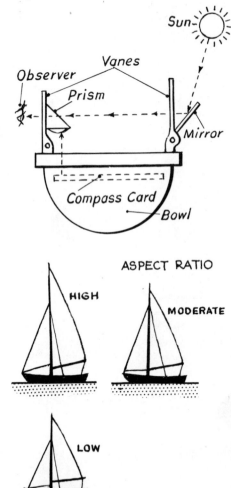

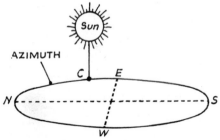

13

B

Back and Fill
A method of alternately filling and then backing the sails when there is insufficient seaway for tacking or manoeuvring in constricted waters.

Backsplice
Prevents reeving through a block. Also tidies up the end of a rope. To start, unlay a few inches of rope and tie a crown knot (1) pull it taut, then tuck each strand next to it and under the next one. (2) Repeat this all round until splice is complete.

Backwinded
A headsail, sheeted too tight, spills its wind into the back of the mainsail which is then backwinded. Backwinding can also be caused by the sail of another boat.

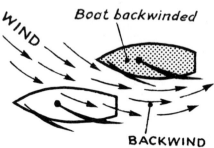

Bag
A sail 'bags' when the leech is taut and the canvas is slack.

Baggywrinkle
Padding made up of yarn and wrapped round shrouds to prevent chafing of the mainsail. Plastic tubing is usually used now.

Backstays
Wire ropes which take up the forward strain of the mast; they are led from the masthead to points on either side of the vessel well aft.

In traditional craft frequently adjustable (running backstays) but modern Bermudan-rigged yachts have them leading from the masthead to either quarter, or often a single backstay leading to the stern.

Bailer

A utensil used for removing water from an open boat; a necessary part of a boat's equipment, including a bucket. Some boats have a self-bailer installed with a trap-door arrangement.

HAND BAILER

Pull handle to close and lock — - -> Trapdoor

Skin

Non-return flap   Out-flow of water

SELF-BAILER

Balance Lug

A small-boat term for a lugsail with its foot laced to a boom and yard. Well suited to quiet waters. Standing and dipping lugs are variations. See also *Lugsail*.

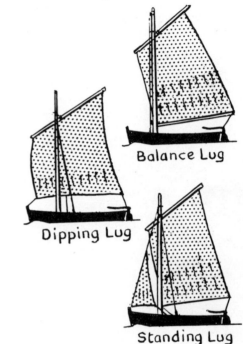

Balance Lug

Dipping Lug

Standing Lug

Ballast

Any heavy substance, such as stone, iron, lead, etc put into or on to a vessel to give it stability. The effect of ballast depends upon its position as well as its amount.

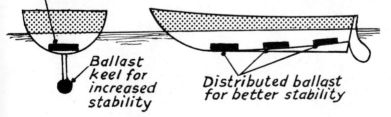

Ballast in bottom

Ballast keel for increased stability

Distributed ballast for better stability

Balloon Jib

A headsail used when running. It is a much safer sail for the single-hander than the spinnaker, as one does not have to alter it when gybing the mainsail.

Beacons

Signals: posts erected onshore, with different shaped topmarks to guide ships, boats, etc.

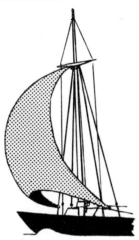

Bare Poles (Under)

A vessel sailing with no sails set, sometimes called 'scudding', when running before a gale.

Beam

(1) The width of a vessel at her widest point. (2) *Abaft the Beam:* anything outside the vessel appearing aft of a line leading athwartships at the widest point. (3) *On the Beam:* anything at right angles to the fore-and-aft line of a vessel.

Battens

Stiffeners made of thin wood or plastic which are slid into pockets sewn into the leech of the mainsail, to help the sail set properly.

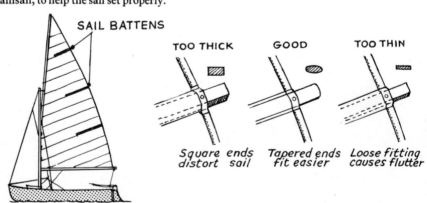

SAIL BATTENS

TOO THICK   GOOD   TOO THIN

Square ends distort sail   Tapered ends fit easier   Loose fitting causes flutter

Bear Away
To put up the helm and turn boat's head away from the wind.

Bear Down (on)
To approach something from windward.

Bearers
(1) Small beams supporting cabin sole or cockpit floor. (2) The timbers fitted fore and aft in boats as the engine bed.

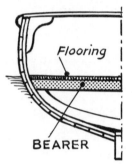

Flooring

BEARER

Beating
Beating to windward is to make progress against the wind, or beating on alternate tacks.

BEATING
(Starb'd Tack)

Wind

Bearing
The bearing of an object or place is the *angle* that the direction of the object or place makes with the meridian, and is relative to the vessel's course.

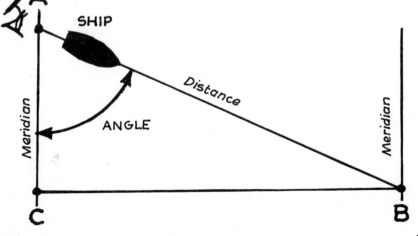

A

SHIP

Meridian

Distance

ANGLE

Meridian

C

B

Beaufort Wind Scale
A table recording the velocity of winds and
their speeds.

Beaufort Number	Description	Speed in knots*	Height of sea in feet †	Deep sea criteria
0	**Calm**	less than 1	—	Sea mirror-smooth.
1	**Light air**	1–3	$\frac{1}{4}$	Small wavelets like scales, no crests.
2	**Light breeze**	4–6	$\frac{1}{2}$	Small wavelets still short but more pronounced. Crests glassy and do not break.
3	**Gentle breeze**	7–10	2	Large wavelets. Crests begin to break. Foam is glassy.
4	**Moderate breeze**	11–16	$3\frac{1}{2}$	Small waves becoming longer; more frequent white horses.
5	**Fresh breeze**	17–21	6	Moderate waves, and longer; many white horses.
6	**Strong breeze**	22–27	$9\frac{1}{2}$	Large waves begin to form; white crests more extensive.
7	**Near gale**	28–33	$13\frac{1}{2}$	Sea heaps up; white foam blown in streaks.
8	**Gale**	34–40	18	Moderately high waves of greater length; crests begin to form spindrift. Foam blown in well-marked streaks.
9	**Strong gale**	41–47	23	High waves; dense streaks of foam. Crests begin to roll over.
10	**Storm**	48–55	29	Very high waves with long overhanging crests. Surface of sea becomes white with great patches of foam. Visibility affected.
11	**Violent storm**	56–63	37	Exceptionally high waves. Sea completely covered with foam.
	Hurricane	64+		The air is filled with spray and visibility seriously affected.

* Measured at the height of 33ft (10m) above sea-level.
† In the open sea remote from land.

Beeblock

A half-block of wood with a sheave through which a reefing pennant is rove, and fastened flat against a boom or spar.

Belay

(1) To secure a rope round a belaying pin, bollard, or cleat, without tying a knot. (2) *Belaying pin:* a pin or bolt of wood placed in a pin-rail for the belaying of halyards, etc.

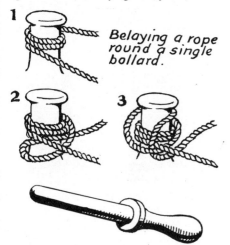

Belaying a rope round a single bollard.

Belly Band

Strip of canvas sewn across large sails to strengthen them for reef points.

Bend

(1) To fasten together two ends of a rope. (2) A general sea term for fastening anything. (3) To lie over under press of canvas when sailing (to heel). (4) You also bend on sails.

Common Bend

Bermuda Rigged

Sailing craft fitted with a triangular sail with no throat or gaff. The head of the sail goes to the masthead and the foot to a boom while the luff is kept to the mast by runners in a slide track. Sometimes called 'the leg of mutton' or 'Marconi rig'.

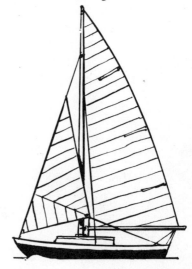

Berthing

When berthing a motor-boat at a mooring quay or landing stage, approach at an angle. With engine going ahead and using correct rudder, boat will swing into position. Have bow rope handy.

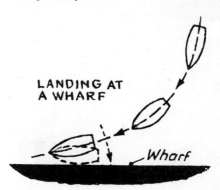

LANDING AT A WHARF

Wharf

With a sailing-boat note must be taken of the wind direction and condition when approaching a landing-stage. If the wind is blowing parallel with the shore, the final approach can be made between a reach and close-hauled.

Bight
(1) A loop in a length of rope. (2) Curve of a coast or river, a bay.

A Bight

Bilge(s)
The rounded lower part of the hull where the side and bottom planks meet. The deepest part inside the hull.

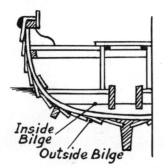

Inside Bilge
Outside Bilge

Bilge Pump
Used for pumping out waste liquid from the bilges. These range from the hand pump for small craft to the electrical or gear type pump used on larger boats.

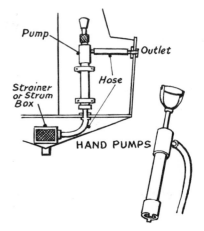

Pump
Outlet
Hose
Strainer or Strum Box
HAND PUMPS

Binnacle
The fixed case and stand in which the steering compass is housed. It has components that minimize compass deviation.

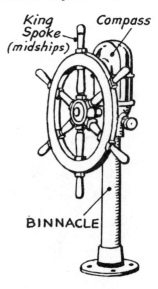

King Spoke (midships)
Compass
BINNACLE

Bitts
A pair of small posts, or iron heads, on deck for fastening warps to or supporting the stock of the bowsprit in smaller craft. Other bitts are used for belaying.

Blanket
To take the wind out of the sails of another vessel, by sailing to windward of her.

Bleeper
A distress signal unit operated by battery and aerial, which emits a continuous signal—monitored by aircraft. It gives them your position should you need help in an emergency. Useful for small craft without a radio.

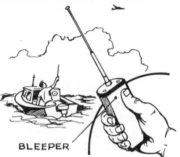

BLEEPER

Block
Originally a block of wood with a hole in it for a rope to reeve through. Modern blocks are sheaved and made of metal. It is used to change the lead of a rope, as in raising a heavy object that cannot be conveniently reached; used in rigging and tackle.

Blue Peter
The 'P' flag of the International Code of Signals denoting the departure of a vessel, or the start of a race. Flown from the forepart of the rigging, it is a blue flag with a white square in the centre.

Blue Water Sailing
Those yachtsmen who prefer to take their boats out to open sea rather than cruise around coastal waters.

Boat's Bag
A canvas bag containing the following articles: hammer, chisel, tingle, palm, and needle for small repairs, twine, copper nails, marline spike, tallow, etc. For sea-boats it is important to have these items for quick repair work.

Boat-Hook
A hook or spike at the end of a pole; used for fending off or holding a boat alongside, or recovering anything from the water.

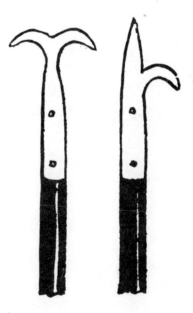

Boat Pulling
To handle a boat under oars is an art acquired by constant practice. In pulling do not let your arms do all the work, but lean back with your feet together on the stretcher and your back straight and let the weight of your body do the work.

Boat Trailer

Two-wheeled trailer used for towing small boat, dinghy, etc behind a car. It is important to select the right trailer for your boat. Besides the weight of the boat, you must also add the weight of an outboard motor, extra fittings, and other equipment. If the trailer weighs over 2cwt (51kg) it should have brakes, and must be strong and well sprung. Make sure the towing-bracket is in good order, and has a rear light. A trailer must be insured.

Bob Stay

The stay from the stempost to the tip of the bowsprit, to counteract the upward strain of the forestays.

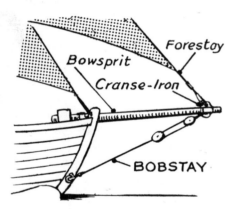

Bollards

Timber or metal posts seen on the sides of docks, quays, and piers, etc for securing ropes to; belaying a rope round a bollard.

Boltropes

The ropes sewn onto the edges of a sail for strengthening purposes. Always sewn on the port side of the sail, which helps when you are changing sails in the dark.

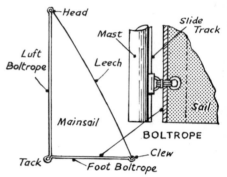

Bolts

On shipboard there are various bolts which may be screwed into almost any part of a boat to lead ropes through, or make timbers fast.

Bonnet
Additional canvas laced to sailfoot to increase its area, for the purpose of gathering extra wind.

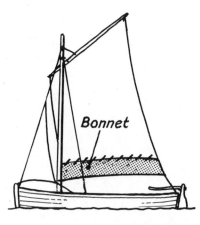

Booby Hatch
A sliding wooden hatch or covered entrance leading down to the cabin of a small boat.

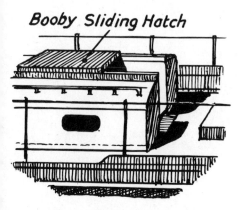

Boom
A long spar, or pole, as it is sometimes called, run out for the purpose of extending the bottom of a particular sail, as the *jib*-boom, the *spinnaker*-boom, etc.

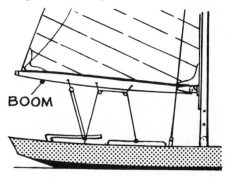

Boomkin
(or Bumpkin). A short spar extending either beyond the bow for fore tacks to be hauled down to, or beyond the stern, to carry a mizzen sheet lead.

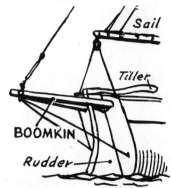

Boot Topping
A strip of very hard-wearing paint along a yacht's sides betwixt wind and water, usually a different colour from that of the topsides and the anti-fouling which it demarcates.

Borrowing
To approach closely either to land or to wind, when it is safe to do so.

23

Bottle Screw

A turnbuckle with a single or double screw, some have a swivel at one end. Used for setting up ends of standing rigging, guard rails, etc; for providing tension, particularly in shrouds.

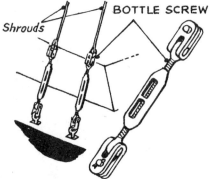

Bottom Boards

These are fitted inside the bottom of pulling boats, to keep the weight from the planking, and to provide a walking surface between the thwarts.

Bows

The hull surfaces in the forepart, which are rounded to meet the stem (port bow and starboard bow).

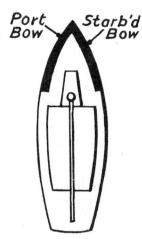

Bowsprit

A spar running out from vessel's stem to which forestays and bobstays are fastened. Often seen in schooners to enable them to carry more sail; it has many disadvantages.

Box the Compass

Repeating the points of the compass in order starting from any point, going full circle, N, N by E, etc.

Brace

(1) A rope attached to boom or yard-arm for trimming sail. In square-rigged vessels the braces trim the yards horizontally. (2) Temporary pieces of timber used in boatbuilding, such as fore-and-aft braces, cross braces, etc.

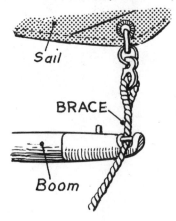

Brails
Ropes for gathering up the foot and leeches of a fore-and-aft sail for furling.

Breakwater
(1) Sometimes seen on the forepart of a deck; a washboard which deflects the water and helps to keep the cockpit dry. (2) Harbour wall.

Breaming
The removal of marine growth from a vessel's bottom by burning and scraping.

Breasthook
A v-shaped piece of timber placed across the stem, to unite the bows and strengthen the forepart of the boat.

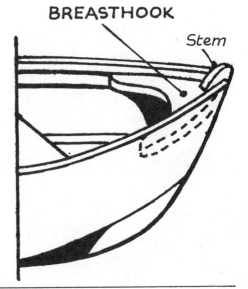

BREASTHOOK

Stem

Breast Ropes
Short mooring lines holding vessel close into quay.

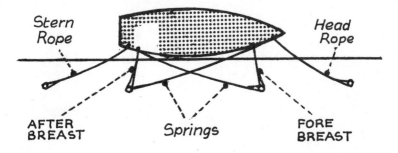

SHORELINES OF A YACHT SECURED ALONGSIDE A JETTY

Stern Rope

Head Rope

AFTER BREAST

Springs

FORE BREAST

25

Breastwork

The rails and stanchions athwart a vessel, across or at the end of a deck.

Breezes

Sea and land breezes are local winds, caused by the unequal heating of land and water. During the day the land becomes warmer than the sea, resulting in low pressure over the land. This causes the heavier and denser air over the sea to flow towards the land. At night these conditions are reversed. Sea and land breezes are most frequent during settled weather.

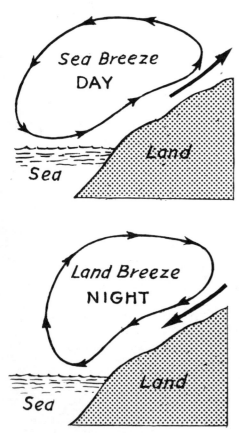

Bridle

Mooring cable. A length of rope secured at both ends and controlled from its centre by another rope.

Bring To

To check the course of a sailing vessel by luffing and bringing her up to the wind.

Broaching To

To 'broach to' means to slew round up into the wind when running before the wind; very dangerous as end of boom and clew of mainsail can sink into a following sea, often resulting in a capsize or inadvertent gybe. NB Do not confuse with 'to broach' which means to break open, ie to broach a cask.

Boom dips in water, thus causing loss of rudder control.

Broadside

The whole length of a vessel's side above the water-line.

Buckler

A piece of wood plugging the hawsehole to prevent water entering when the vessel pitches.

Bulkhead

Upright partition dividing a boat into compartments; also adds stiffening to the hull.

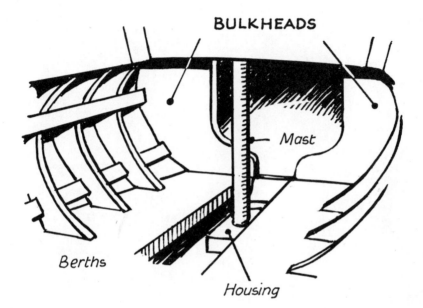

BULKHEADS

Mast

Berths

Housing

Bullrope

Any length of rope which is used to prevent something from chafing, eg, a rope led from end of bowsprit attached to a mooring buoy to keep the buoy from bumping against the vessel's stem.

Bunt

(1) The middle part, cavity, or belly of a sail; the part of a furled sail which is at the centre of the boom or yard. (2) *Buntline:* a rope passing from the footrope of a square sail up to the yard and thence to the deck; used in hauling the sail up to the yard.

BUNT

Boom   BUNT, *furled and reefed.*

Buoy

A float permanently anchored to a certain spot. Of two kinds: (1) mooring buoys—for ships to secure to; (2) marker buoys—used for marking isolated dangers and navigable channels.

Mooring Buoys

PORT HAND BUOYS

STARBOARD HAND BUOYS

WRECK BUOYS

MIDDLE GROUND BUOYS

Pass either way

ISOLATED DANGER BUOYS

Pass either side

LANDFALL *or* FAIRWAY BUOYS

Pass either side

Buoyage System

The internationally agreed system of marker buoys. Coming from seaward, port-hand marks are generally red and can-shaped; starboard-hand marks black or green and cone-shaped. From 1977 the new IALA system has been progressively adopted. This incorporates both the traditional 'lateral' and the French 'quadrantal' systems.

Burgee

Small pointed or swallow-tailed flag used by yachts, yacht clubs, etc. The burgee marks the club to which a yacht belongs. The International Code contains two burgees, letters A and B. Also used as a wind indicator.

Redwing Club, London, England

Royal Akarana Y.C. New Zealand

Butt Joints

The ends of planks, plates, etc. The joint where two planks in a strake meet. Also named the thick end of a spar.

Buttock

(1) The curved under-portion of the stern; the part between the transom and the bilge, which extends from the sheer strake to the keel. (2) The 'Buttock Line' as used in boat-building plans, is a continual vertical section through one of the buttocks.

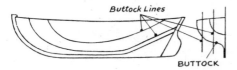

Buttock Lines

BUTTOCK

By The Wind

Sailing close-hauled, to within about six points of the wind.

C

Cabin

Crew or passengers' compartment on a vessel. The accommodation below deck in yachts.

Callipers

Compasses or dividers, for measuring or setting off distances; used in chart work.

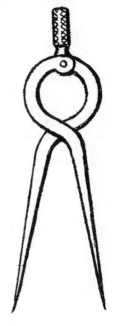

Camber

(1) The convex surface of a deck that sheds the water. (2) Sail camber is the curvature that a sail should have. Care should be taken that this is correct.

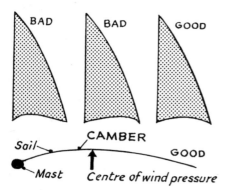

Canvas

Made of hemp, flax, or cotton fibres; it is used for making sails, awnings, and various other kinds of covers. It is sold in bolts. A bolt measures 42yd (38½m).

Cap

(1) The fitting over the head of a mast for retaining the next above it. (2) A ring at the end of a spar. (3) A covering of tarred canvas at the end of a rope.

Camping

Camping on board in a small boat can be quite possible with a little improvisation. Hold up the boom with its topping lift, and stretch a sheet of canvas over it, with a pair of sheer legs at the afterend to give extra support. With a sleeping bag you have a shelter. For extra head-room give the gooseneck a second position up the mast. Moor the boat with the shelter and its bow into the wind, and the end tightly closed.

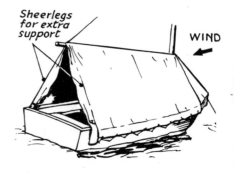

Capping Rail

The thin wood that covers the gunwale around a boat.

Capsize

The overturning of a boat. The sketch shows how to get a small boat upright. Warning: should this happen never try to swim for it, always stay with your boat, which is more easily seen than a swimmer.

RIGHTING A CAPSIZED BOAT

Careen
To turn a vessel or boat on one side for cleaning or caulking, etc.

Carlings
Short beams running between transverse beams fore and aft. They are joined to the end beams of deck openings and support the coamings of the cockpit, hatches, and cabin sides.

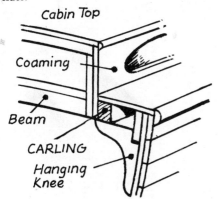

Cabin Top

Coaming

Beam

CARLING

Hanging Knee

Carrying Rudder
Term used when, for any reason, the rudder instead of steering a steady course, shows a tendency to wander away from it. To counteract this tendency the helmsman may have to keep a small angle on the rudder to bring the vessel's head up to the wind, because she tends to fall off.

Carry Away
To break or part.

Carry Way (On)
To continue moving through the water although engine is stopped and sails not drawing. Luffing up into the wind and sea soon takes 'way' off a boat.

Carvel
A boat constructed with its planking flush, presenting a smooth surface. Most yachts are carvel-built.

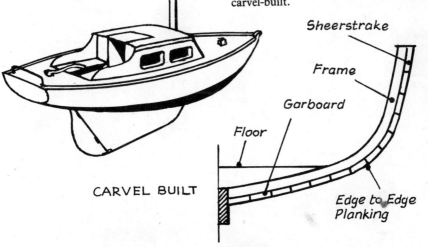

Sheerstrake

Frame

Garboard

Floor

CARVEL BUILT

Edge to Edge Planking

Cast Off
To let go a mooring, to loosen or release a rope.

Catamaran
A craft consisting of a deck on which the helmsman and crew sit supported between two narrow hulls.

Catenary
The curve formed by a rope or chain suspended freely between two points of suspension, such as the curve of a tow-rope when a vessel is towed, or the cable of a vessel at anchor, where it helps to withstand any sudden stress.

Cathead
A projecting piece of timber or metal near the bow of a vessel, to which the anchor is hoisted and secured.

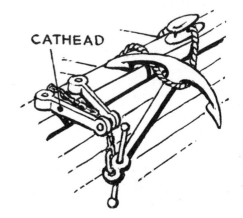

CATHEAD

Cat Boat
A one-masted sailing-boat having its mast stepped well forward, carrying a single fore-and-aft sail extended by a gaff and boom. A boat with a centreboard, not suitable for rough waters.

CAT BOAT

Caulking

Filling the seams of planking with oakum using a caulking iron and mallet, or a ladle filled with marine glue, to make a boat watertight.

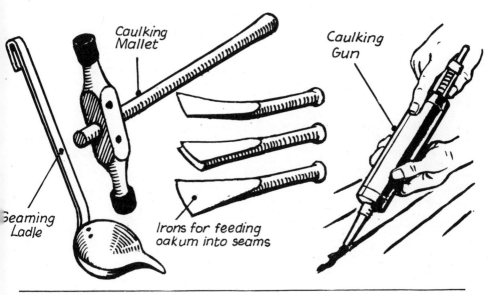

Caulking Mallet

Caulking Gun

Seaming Ladle

Irons for feeding oakum into seams

Cavitation

Excessive vibration caused by poor propeller design, faulty positioning, or damaged propeller. It entails severe loss of thrust.

Celestial Navigation

This deals with finding one's position by means of the sun, moon, and stars; used mainly for offshore and ocean cruising. With the use of a sextant and the aid of a Navigational Table, a fix can be obtained by measuring the angle of any celestial body at a certain time.

Celestial Sphere

The imaginary spherical surface enclosing all the heavenly bodies, which has the planet Earth as its centre.

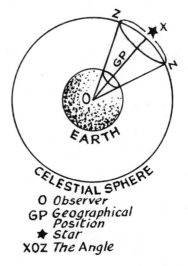

EARTH

CELESTIAL SPHERE

O Observer
GP Geographical Position
★ Star
XOZ The Angle

33

Chafing Gear
Matting or spunyarn put up on rigging or spars to prevent chafing.

Chainplates
(or Channel Plates). The metal bands on a vessel's sides, usually inboard, to which the shrouds are fastened.

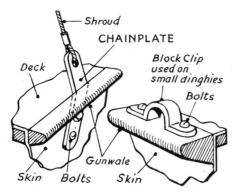

Channel
(1) The deep part of a strait, estuary, or river, where the current or tide is strongest; especially a navigable passage between the shoal parts. (2) *Channel-ways* that convey water off any part of a vessel.

Channels
Points on the sides of a boat for shrouds to hold the mast steady.

Chart
A detailed sea map with coast outlines, rocks, shoals, etc for the use of navigators. Charts are basically of three main types: *passage charts* that embrace a comparatively large part of an ocean, or the entire ocean; *coastal charts* showing the extent of a coastline with its contiguous waters; and *harbour plans*.

Chart Datum
A low-water level below which the tide seldom falls, and is used for the datum line of the area on that particular chart.

Chart-House
The space set apart for the use of the navigator, and the stowing of his navigational instruments.

Chart Symbols
The principal symbols used on navigation charts. A complete list of them may be obtained through any Admiralty Chart Agency.

Cheeks
(1) Knee-pieces fastened to a mast to support the cross-trees. (2) The two sides of a block.

Chine
The line formed by the intersection of the sides and bottom of a V-bottom boat. The commonest method of construction is in plywood which is glued and screwed, or nailed to lengthwise members. It offers an advantage for high-speed motor-boats and is much easier to build than the round bilge type.

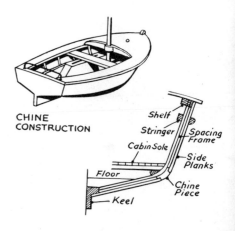

Chiplog
A device for measuring the speed of a vessel; usually a triangular board, weighted on one edge and attached to a line (the log-line). That is 'streamed' out from a reel held by a man on board. The 'log' remaining stationary in the water. The log-line is divided by knots, the equal spaces between which bear the same relation to a nautical mile as the time during which the line is run out bears to an hour.

Chock-A-Block
(or Two Blocks). When two blocks are brought together in a tackle and no further purchase is possible.

Chocks
(1) Wedges used to prevent anything moving when boat is rolling. (2) To make boat fast on chocks. (3) A horn-shaped metal fixing, usually seen near the gunwale, for ropes or hawsers to pass between when towing or mooring, etc.

Chronometer
The vessel's time-measuring instrument for navigational purposes, used for fixing longitude at sea, etc.

Clamp
A fore-and-aft plank fitted inside and fastened to frames of small craft; to act as a bearer for a beam or joint.

CHRONOMETER

Clapper
A pivoted fitting between the jaws of a gaff to prevent that from jamming when hauled down the mast.

Class
Boats that conform to a certain formula and design, such as the boats and yachts used for racing purposes. Racing yachts are grouped according to their measurements.

Clawing Off
To beat to windward, as from a lee shore, getting away by sailing as close to the wind as possible while still making good way.

Cleat

A device made of wood or metal, having two arms, around which turns may be taken with a line or rope so as to hold securely and yet be readily released, usually bolted to a deck or mast, etc.

Clench or Clinch

(1) To fasten (rope) with a half-hitch. (2) To secure nail or rivet by driving point sideways when through two overlapping strakes.

Clew

The lower after corner of a fore-and-aft sail.

Clinker Built

A method of building a boat in which the planks overlap downwards and are fastened with clinched copper nails.

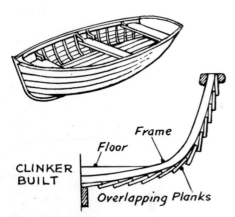

CLINKER BUILT

Clinometer

An instrument for measuring angle of heel or pitch; located on the compass binnacle.

Clipper Bow

The type of overhang bow in sailing yachts which is concave, whereas that of the spoon bow is convex, and most common.

Clips

An appliance that clasps, grips, or holds fast. Clip hooks—sometimes called Sister Hooks—are a combination of two hooks, joined together facing each other. When closed together they form an eye, used for clipping a rope. *Sheet Clips* are metal implements fixed to the deck in sailing boats on which to jam a sheet.

Close-Hauled

Sailing as close to the wind as possible, that is toward the direction from which the wind blows.

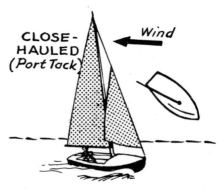

CLOSE-HAULED (Port Tack)

Wind

Close-Reefed

When all the reefs are taken in as much as possible to reduce the area of sail.

Cloth
A length of canvas used to form part of a sail.

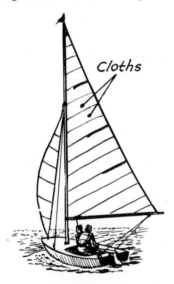

Cloths

Clothes for Boating
Protective clothing is necessary in an open boat and spare clothing should always be carried in a waterproof bag; it is colder afloat than ashore. Footwear should be chosen with care as falls are dangerous aboard a boat. Smooth rubber soles are slippery when wet and should be avoided, rope-soled shoes are the best. Never wear gumboots on board.

Cloud Formations
An important element in sailing is keeping a weather eye open for sudden squalls or thunderstorms, when winds can be violent and dangerous. Look for the following signs which usually prove reliable:
(1) *Cirrus*: known as 'mare's tails' wispy white clouds, usually indicate rain and wind within 24 hours.
(2) *Cirro-cumulus*: this is known as the mackerel sky and means rain is about.
(3) *Cirro-stratus*: a halo around either moon or sun frequently indicates bad weather the next day.

(4) *Cumulo-nimbus*: this cloud on a high level indicates squalls and thunderstorms, usually of short duration. The winds can be violent and dangerous.

Clubbing
(or Dredging). Drifting stern foremost down a fast current with an anchor dropped short; a method used to bring a vessel to her berth.

Club-Hauling
An emergency measure used when trying to claw off a dangerous lee shore in rough weather if heavy seas prevent the vessel coming about. A kedge warp and anchor are prepared. The anchor is dropped just before going about. As soon as it 'bites' take a turn round the bitts and put the helm down. The moment the vessel's head is safely through the wind the warp is severed. Obviously the number of times you can use this tactic is limited to the number of warps and anchors you have to spare.

Club Topsail
A kind of gaff topsail, used mostly by yachts having a fore-and-aft rig. It has a short 'club' or 'jack yard' to increase its spread.

Clump
A concrete slab to which a mooring chain is attached. To this chain is shackled the buoy rope or chain.

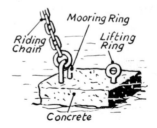

Riding Chain   Mooring Ring   Lifting Ring

Concrete

Coach-Roof

The cabin top above deck level giving additional head-room in small boats.

Coaming

Raised edge around the hatches of a vessel or boat to keep water out.

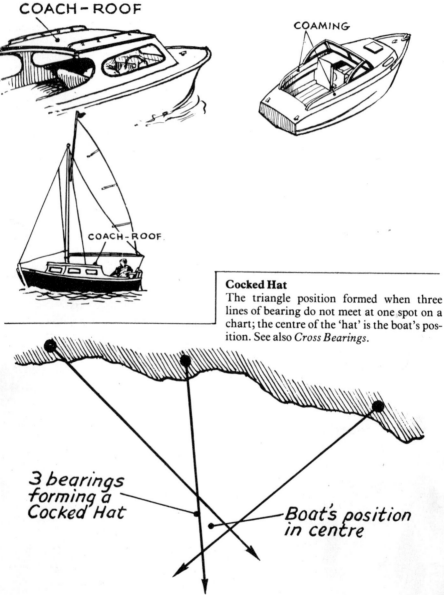

COACH - ROOF

COAMING

COACH-ROOF

Cocked Hat

The triangle position formed when three lines of bearing do not meet at one spot on a chart; the centre of the 'hat' is the boat's position. See also *Cross Bearings*.

3 bearings forming a Cocked Hat

Boat's position in centre

Cockpit
Generally an area aft of the cabin, below the usual deck level to form a well where the helmsman sits.

COCKPIT

Code Flag
The code flag and *Answering Pendant* indicates that the International Code of Signals is being used.

Coiling a Rope
To coil down a rope, lay clockwise in rings called flakes, each one over the other to allow the rope to run freely. If one end still fast, capsize the whole coil ready for use.

Coir
A material for cordage, matting, etc consisting of the prepared fibre of the coconut.

Collar Knot
An eye formed in the bight or bend of a shroud, or stay, to go over the masthead and down on to the hounds, for fitting shrouds to a small mast.

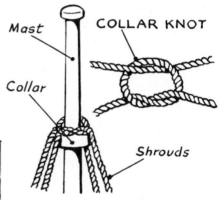

Mast

COLLAR KNOT

Collar

Shrouds

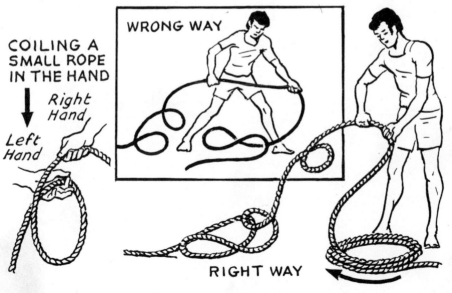

COILING A SMALL ROPE IN THE HAND

Right Hand

Left Hand

WRONG WAY

RIGHT WAY

Collision

The Board of Trade issue instructions for the prevention of collisions at sea, which constitute the 'Rules of the Road'.

Commodore

The presiding officer of a yacht club.

Companion Hatch

A fixed or sliding cover over entrance to cabin. The *Companion Way* is the ladder or stairway leading below.

Compass

(Magnetic). The compass used by navigators. It comprises a magnetic needle or needles attached to a circular card within a bowl mounted on gimbals. The card is divided into 33 points, or 360 degrees, $11\frac{1}{4}$ degrees equalling 1 point, and is housed in a binnacle. Used for determining the magnetic meridian by which the vessel is navigated when a gyro is not fitted. All vessels must have two of these compasses on board. A compass is named according to its position in the vessel, eg *Standard Compass*, which is usually in the highest part of the vessel, the *Steering Compass*, used by the helmsman, etc. *Hand-bearing Compass*, in small boats where the compass is mounted in front of the wheel it is not possible to take bearings of landmarks abaft the beam, therefore a hand-bearing compass is used. It is fitted with a rotating azimuth mirror from which bearings can be read off.

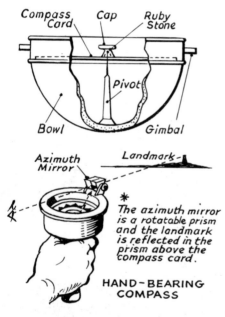

Compass Card

The circular card or dial of a marine compass, which is marked off in points or degrees, and to which the magnetic needles are fixed. The *Compass Rose* is found on charts: this is a reproduction of the compass card with the cardinal points and the 360 degrees ring marked thereon, allied with the magnetic variation arrow—not to be confused with compass deviation.

Compass Course

The angle cos the vessel's track makes with the direction of the magnetic needle. It may be affected by variation and deviation, and consequently must be corrected for both in order to obtain the true course.

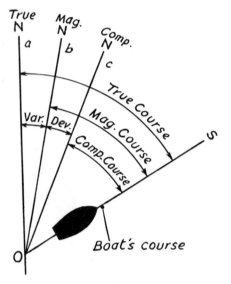

Boat's course

Compass Error

Is the sum of the deviation and the variation. When both are easterly or both are westerly they are added together. If one is easterly and the other westerly, they are subtracted one from the other and the error is called by the name of the larger.

Cone

A black, conical-shaped canvas used in bad weather as a gale-warning signal.

Constant Bearing

A bearing that remains the same; should the bearing of another vessel not alter it indicates a risk of collision.

Cordage

Ropes and cords in general; especially ropes in the rigging of a sailing vessel.

Counter

The underside of the overhang of a stern.

Counter

Course

(1) The direction, by compass, in which the vessel is travelling. There are three courses as shown. (2) A sail bent to the lower yard of any square-rigged mast.

Course Protractor

A celluloid disc marked in compass points and degrees, with a movable arm pivoted at centre of disc. Replaces the parallel rulers.

Cradle

(1) Framework used to support a boat during construction or repairs. Also used in the launching of a vessel. (2) A platform used for working over the side of a vessel.

Cramps

Various types of cramps are used in boatbuilding for holding parts together. The number required depends on the size of boat. In some cases it is necessary to use wooden cramps which can be made quite easily.

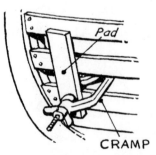

Pad

CRAMP

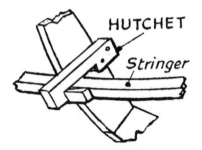

HUTCHET

Stringer

Clinker Method

GRIPE

Cranse Iron
A ring fitted at the end of a bowsprit to take the shrouds and bobstay. Also prevents the spar from splintering.

Cringle
A rope loop containing a metal thimble worked in the leech and clew of a sail for another rope to pass through.

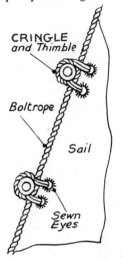

CRINGLE and Thimble

Boltrope

Sail

Sewn Eyes

Cross Bearings
The bearings of two stationary objects taken from the same place: used to fix the position of a vessel that is close to shore. See also *Cocked Hat.*

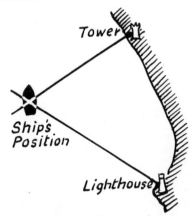

Tower

Ship's Position

Lighthouse

Cross-Piece
A piece of timber or iron connecting two bitts.

Cross Seas
Caused through a change of wind which builds up a sea in a different direction to one left by an earlier wind; makes the sea choppy.

Cruiser Mast
Used on modern motor-cruisers, the mast carries a navigational light, a club pennant, and signal flags.

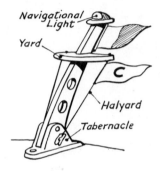

Navigational Light

Yard

Halyard

Tabernacle

Crutch

(1) A supporting trestle used in yachts to take the weight of the main boom off the topping lift, when not in use. (2) A portable metal rowlock which supports the oar on the gunwale of a row-boat.

Current

A flow of surface water. 'Setting' is its direction; 'drift' is the rate at which it flows.

Current Tables

Charts giving times of slack water, and the direction, times and velocities of currents.

Cutter

A sailing vessel with one mast. The modern type of cutter has a mainsail with two sails set forward of the mast with the inner and outer forestays almost parallel. The older type has the forestays converging towards the mast, with two head-sails set one above the other.

Cutwater

The curved portion of a vessel's stem which cleaves the water as she moves.

Cyclonic

A disturbance of the atmosphere, characterized by decrease of barometric pressure toward the centre and by winds directed spirally inward. The winds circulate anticlockwise in the northern hemisphere and clockwise in the southern.

D

Dan Buoy

A small buoy with a spar, one end secured to a weight by a mooring rope, used as a marker and easily recoverable.

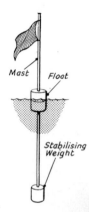

Dandy
A small mizzen sail on a ketch or yawl carried at or near the stern: it is usually triangular.

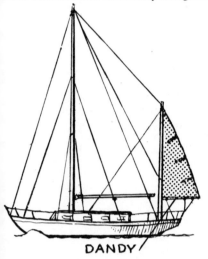

DANDY

Davits
Metal supports used for suspending or lowering vessel's boat. Any projecting arm used for hoisting.

Day Mark
(1) Signals carried by vessels in daylight—details given in 'Rules of the Road' in any nautical almanac. (2) An unlit navigation mark on land.

Deadeyes
Round blocks with three holes through which shroud lanyards are rove; so-named because they are not fitted with a pulley.

Dead Reckoning
The computation of a vessel's place at sea without astronomical observations, solely by distance run and compass course with corrections for drift, leeway, etc. The principal instruments used in navigation by dead reckoning are the chart, the lead, the mariner's compass, and the log.

Deadrise
The angle made between the frame at bottom near keel and a horizontal through line of contact at bottom with keel.

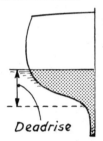

Deadrise

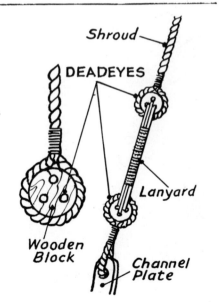

Shroud

DEADEYES

Lanyard

Wooden Block

Channel Plate

Deadwood

Timber used in the build up of forward or after end of keel structure, for the fastening of stem or stern-post and horn timbers, where the rudder is hung.

Deck Canvas

A canvas cut to shape of deck and tacked to deck as a preventive against leaks.

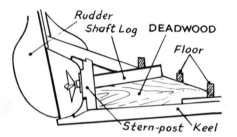

Rudder
Shaft Log DEADWOOD
Floor
Stern-post Keel

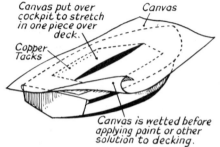

Canvas put over cockpit to stretch in one piece over deck.
Canvas
Copper Tacks
Canvas is wetted before applying paint or other solution to decking.

Deck

A covering of planks extending the full length of a vessel supported by beams, to form both a floor and a covering for the space below it. The various decks are named depending on the type of vessel or craft. Three types of deck are:

(1) *Laid decks*: narrow planks of teak, caulked and payed.

(2) *Double-skin*: planks with a plywood base.

(3) *Tongue and grooved*: deck with a canvas or plastic covering.

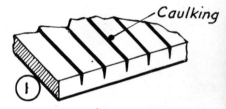

Caulking

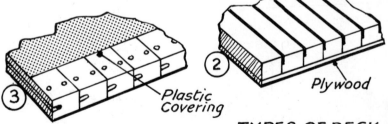

Plastic Covering

Plywood

TYPES OF DECK

Deckhouse

A cabin with its sole at deck level, or countersunk as in small vessels, but above level of the cabin sole throughout the rest of the accommodation.

Deep

(1) An area of deep water between stretches of comparative shoal. (2) An unmarked graduation of the hand lead line (ie, between the 'marks').

Departure

Is the distance made good by the vessel due east or due west in nautical miles. To find the difference of longitude consult the Traverse Tables.

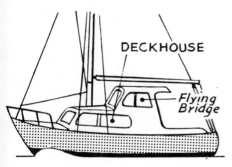

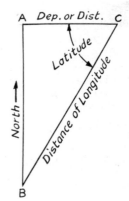

Deck Log

A small log book in which is recorded all alterations of course, speed, weather changes, times, or any event as they occur.

Declination

The declination of a celestial body, for instance the sun, is the angular distance north and south from the extended plane of the earth's equator.

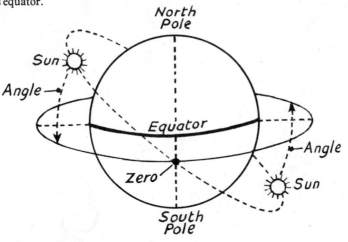

47

Deviation

Is the angle between the magnetic meridian and the compass meridian. Easterly deviation: North end of compass is deflected to the east of the magnetic meridian. Westerly deviation: North end of compass is deflected to the west of the magnetic meridian. This is caused by the presence of iron, steel, and other magnetic objects, such as iron rails, stanchions, stays. All these should be kept as far away from the compass as possible.

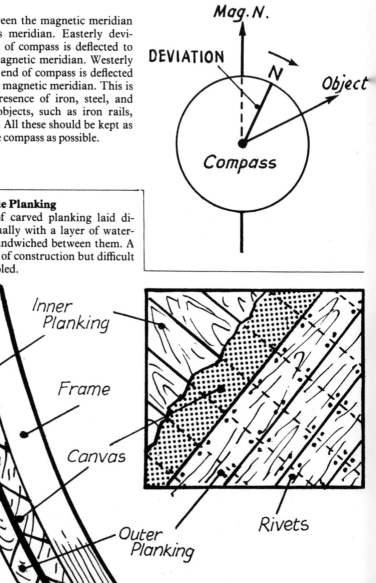

Diagonal Double Planking

A double skin of carved planking laid diagonally and usually with a layer of waterproof material sandwiched between them. A very strong form of construction but difficult to repair when holed.

Inner Planking

Frame

Canvas

Outer Planking

Rivets

Dinghy

A small rowing or sailing boat varying from 8 to 16ft (2.5 to 5m) in length; used for rowing, racing, fishing and general purposes.

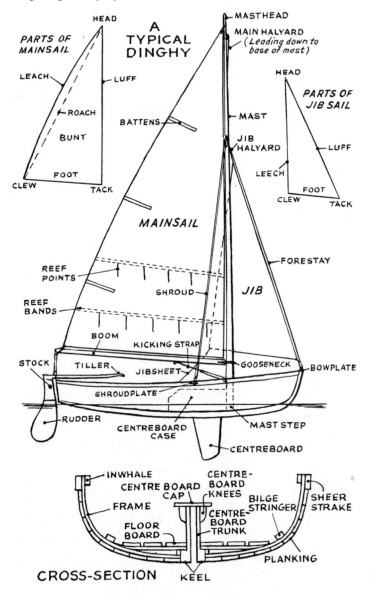

Dip
(or 'Dip of the Horizon'). The angular depression of the seen or visible horizon below the true or natural horizon; the angle at the eye of an observer between a horizontal line and a tangent drawn from the eye to the surface of the ocean.

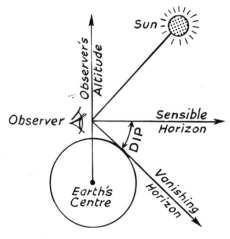

Dipping Lugsail
A sail carried on a short spar made fast before the mast; the sail must be lowered when going about and set again every time a boat carrying it changes her tack.

Displacement
The weight of water displaced by a vessel; this weight being equal to the weight of the vessel (1 ton = 2,240lb (1016kg)).

Distress Signals
No explanation required. They are fully detailed in Annex IV of The International Regulations for Preventing Collisions at Sea.

Ditty Bag
A sailor's sewing kit, contains scissors, needles, cotton, etc for clothes mending.

Dodger
Screen of canvas rigged to shelter the cockpit.

Doghouse
The raised deckhouse that gives all round visibility, usually at aft end of cabin.

Dog Shores
Wooden props used to hold a vessel firmly, and prevent her moving, while the blocks are knocked away before launching.

Doldrums
A part of the ocean near the equator abounding in calms, and baffling winds, which sometimes prevent all progress for weeks.

Dolphin
(1) A mooring post on a wharf or beach to secure a vessel. (2) A permanent fender around a heavy boat below the gunwale. *Dolphin Striker*: the small perpendicular spar below a bowsprit and jib-boom acting as a lead for an extra bob stay.

Dory
A small, strong, lugsail dory, flat-bottomed, double-ended sailing- or rowing-boat used for pleasure sailing or fishing.

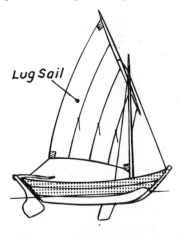

Lug Sail

Double Tide
One tide following another at each flood, which is caused by the main current coming in from two different directions.

Downhaul
A rope to haul down, or to assist in hauling down, a sail; as, a staysail *downhaul*, etc. Anything down from aloft. Also used to stop the boom flying up.

Dowse
To take, or haul down a sail in haste.

Draught
The maximum underwater depth of a ship.

Doubling the Angle on the Bow
A method of coastal navigation that uses the principle of the equilateral triangle. When approaching a coast where only one identifiable object is visible 'on the bow' a bearing is taken of this object C and the log read. The same course is then maintained until the bearing of the object relative to the ship's head has doubled then the log is read again. After allowing for any tide and leeway the distance run AB will equal the distance off BC at B.

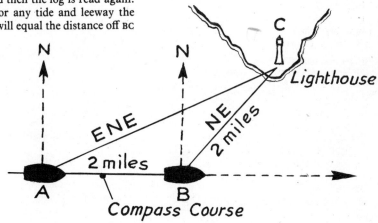

Drift
(1) To float or be driven along with the tide.
(2) The distance through which a current
flows in a given time. (3) The distance between two blocks of a tackle.

Drift Sail
A sail used as a drift anchor. The sail is bent
to a spar, weighed, and immersed during a
storm; it lessens the drift of a vessel.

Drogue
A canvas bag or bucket, used forward as a sea
anchor to steady or check a boat's way in
rough weather. See also *Sea Anchor*.

Dutchman's Log
A way of measuring the speed of a vessel by
throwing a piece of timber or other floating
object overboard forward, so that speed may
be estimated with a stop-watch from the time
taken to pass it.

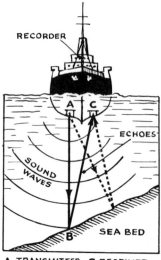

A TRANSMITTER C RECEIVER
OSCILLATOR OSCILLATOR
REFLECTION OF TUG ECHO BY AN
INCLINED SEA BED.

E

Ease
To ease off, to slacken a rope gradually. *To
ease a vessel*, to luff gently to meet a dangerous sea when close-hauled. *Easy*, an order to
go gently, not too fast.

Ebb
The receding of tide water to the ocean:
opposed to *flood*.

Echo Sounder
An apparatus for sounding whereby electrical impulses from a vessel to the sea-bed are
timed on their return, providing a continuous record of depths. The mechanism is
so sensitive that trawlers often use them for
locating the depth of shoals of fish.

RECORDER

Eddy
A circular movement in the water caused by
the meeting of opposite currents.

Elbow in the Hawse
The twisting together of two cables or hawsers, by which a vessel rides at anchor, caused
by her swinging twice the wrong way on an
open hawse.

Engine Bed
The bearers on which the engine rests and is fastened. These in turn are bolted to the floors as stringers to give rigidity.

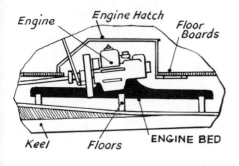

ENGINE BED

Ensign
The distinguishing flag carried by a ship to indicate nationality; flown at the stern or on a halyard at the peak of a gaff sail.

Entrance
The bow, or entire wedgelike forepart of a vessel, below the water-line.

Equator
The imaginary great circle on the earth's surface, everywhere equally distant from the two poles, and dividing the earth's surface into two hemispheres.

Equinox
Time at which the sun crosses the equator and the days and nights are of equal length. This happens twice a year—21 March and 23 September.

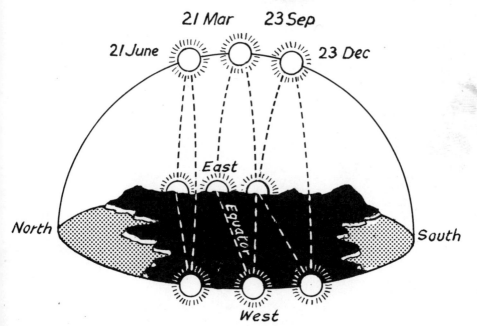

Escutcheon
That part of a vessel's stern on which her name is written.

Even Keel
A boat is on an 'even keel' when in a level or horizontal position.

Eye
A small loop or hole in a splice, an anchor, bolts, or sails, etc.

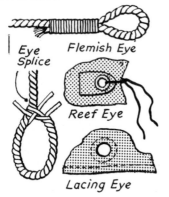

Eye Splice   *Flemish Eye*

Reef Eye

Lacing Eye

Eye Splice
A splice formed by bending a rope's end back and fastening it into the rope, forming a loop or eye.

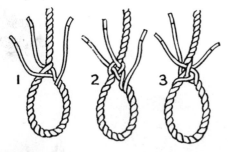

Exposure
(Hypothermia). Cold water affects the metabolism, for instance, oxygen consumption and respiration of a swimmer increase causing fatigue, exhaustion, and shivering. He loses body heat rapidly by conduction,

54

and death can ensue. It is wise to leave the water before becoming chilled. It is not just the man in the water who is affected. Anyone exposed to the combination of cold and damp can suffer these effects.

F

Fairlead
A bolt, ring or any metal fitment attached to the deck of a vessel, through which a rope may be run.

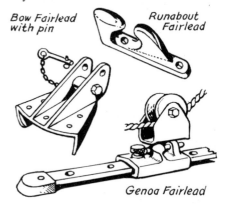

Bow Fairlead with pin

Runabout Fairlead

Genoa Fairlead

Fairway
The part of a harbour or channel which is kept open and unobstructed for the passage of vessels.

Fair Wind
A wind that enables a boat to be sailed from one place to another, without the necessity of tacking.

Fall
The loose end of a rope to be hauled upon, for instance, the fall of a tackle is the rope upon which to pull.

False Keel
An additional keel added to afterend of main keel for protection or for attaching the rudder to.

Fake
A single coil or turn of a rope or cable.

Fashion Pieces
(in boatbuilding). The aftermost timbers secured athwartships that form the shape of the stern.

Fast
Securing a vessel with a hawser, eg headfast and sternfast to bollards, etc. Sometimes termed headrope, sternrope, etc.

Fastenings
The principal fastenings used in boatbuilding are the bolt, nail, and screw. They are either of galvanized iron (for heavier boats) or copper, bronze or some other alloy of copper.

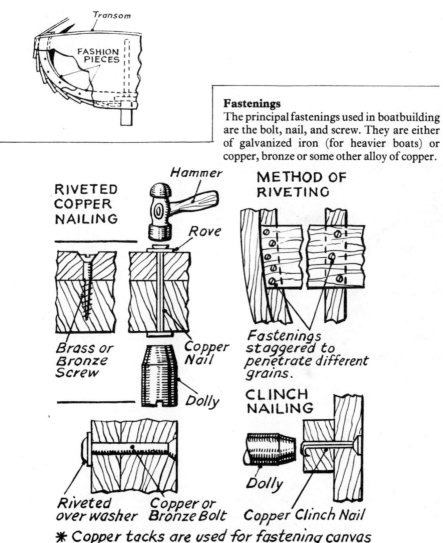

RIVETED COPPER NAILING

Hammer

Rove

METHOD OF RIVETING

Brass or Bronze Screw

Copper Nail

Dolly

Fastenings staggered to penetrate different grains.

CLINCH NAILING

Riveted over washer   Copper or Bronze Bolt   Copper Clinch Nail

Dolly

✳ *Copper tacks are used for fastening canvas*

55

Fathom
A nautical measure 6ft (1.82m); used in the length of ropes, and applied to depths. The space to which a man can extend his arms.

Fathometer
An instrument found on larger yachts. It gives a continuous visual indication of depth.

Faying
To paint wood surfaces before fastening them together.

Feather Edge
A plank sawn diagonally across its section, eg, the planks overlapping in a clinker-built boat.

Fetch
(1) To fetch a *compass*, to take a circuitous route in going to a place. (2) To fetch *away*, to break loose; to roll or slide to leeward. (3) The fetch—distance which the wind travels over the sea with consequent effect on size of waves.

Fibre-glass Boat
A type of hull construction with the whole pattern moulded in a compound of light but strong fibre-glass material.

Fid
(1) A conical wooden pin, used to open the strands of a rope when splicing. (2) An iron pin placed through the hole in the heel of a top mast or bowsprit to lock them in place.

Fiddle
A rack or frame made of wood, used at sea to keep plates, mugs, etc, from falling off the table.

Fenders
Buffers specially made. They are placed where necessary to prevent damage when a vessel comes into contact with another vessel or a wharf. They are portable and taken in when under way.

Rubber Fender

Plaited rope of coir.

Hanging spar to cater for rise and fall of tide.

Canvas bow fender.

MOULDED RUBBER ALL-ROUND FENDERS

Solid rubber fixed with pin.

Hollow moulding fixed with screws

Hollow rubber drilled and screwed in metal strip.

Fiddle Block
A double block with one sheave larger than another for taking two sizes of rope.

Fiferail
An iron rail fitted near or to a mast carrying belaying pins.

Fiferail

Fire Extinguisher
Any boat especially a power-boat that has enclosed space should have one placed in a convenient place, ready for use at all times. Proper maintenance is very important. The danger of explosive vapour surrounding nearly empty tanks is very real indeed. Two types of extinguishers are recommended—carbon dioxide (CO_2), and vapourizing liquid, both effective in restricted places.

1 CARBON DIOXIDE

Draw pin, point at base of fire and pull trigger.

2 VAPORIZING LIQUID

Turn handle to unlock and

discharge at blaze.

First Aid
Every yacht should carry a first-aid kit with the equipment needed to deal with injuries, burns, and scalds, and also a few medicines for dealing with simple complaints. Here are a few essentials: bandages, cotton wool, sticking plaster, disinfectant, pair of scissors, and a pair of tweezers. All crew members should know where the kit is placed ready for use. It is advisable for yachtsmen to carry a first aid manual on board.

Fish
(1) A concave-shaped piece of wood used as a splint to strengthen a damaged mast, yard, or spar, etc. (2) A purchase used to 'fish' the anchor to the side of a vessel.

Fisherman's Staysail
A large topsail set above main staysail, usually seen in schooners, where the foresail is superseded by two staysails, set on the stays between the masts.

Fisherman's Walk
A very small space on the deck of a vessel, a name derived from the deck area of a fishing vessel.

Fish Tail Plates
Metal plates let in to after end of keel and lower end of stern-post, or rudder-post. These plates are fitted each side and through-bolted.

Fix
A navigational term; the intersection of two or more position lines.

Flake
To coil a rope down clear for running.

Flag
A banner indicating the colours of a nation signifying nationality, occupation, or intelligence; used for identification, signalling, etc. A house-flag distinguishes a particular shipping company; yacht clubs fly a member's flag. Sketch shows how to put on a flag.

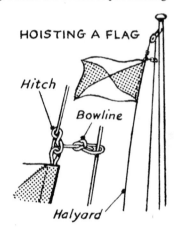

HOISTING A FLAG

Hitch

Bowline

Halyard

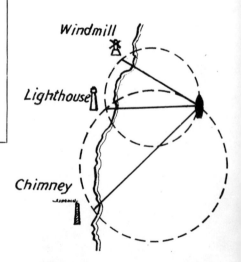

Windmill

Lighthouse

Chimney

Flag Etiquette

Fly your flags correctly; sailors should acquaint themselves with all the rules to avoid any embarrassment. When under way the yacht ensign should be displayed at the main peak of single and two-masted sailing yachts, and at the mizzen peak of three-masted yachts, yawls, and ketches. Single-masted yachts should fly the owner's private signal at the main truck; when at anchor the burgee. It is bad form to fly more than one burgee on the same hoist in any part of the vessel—unless one is using the flags of the international code.

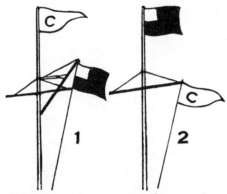

1 **2**

Proper arrangement for yacht club flag poles. If there is no gaff the ensign goes to the masthead — 2. If there is a gaff the ensign is flown there and the club burgee goes to the masthead

Private signal flown forward when underway but club flag should be flown when at anchor.

Red Ensign

Club Pennant

Private

If the boat has a signal mast the owner's flag goes to the masthead, the club flag forward and the yacht ensign aft, when underway

Flare

(1) The bulge of a vessel's sides, upwards and outwards towards a vessel's bows. Designed to prevent water coming on deck. (2) A signal light or distress flare.

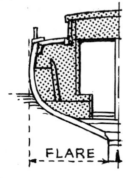

Flashlight

Small rowing- and sail-boats at sea after sunset should have a press-button torch handy to show a white light in sufficient time to draw attention to their position; show flashes of light at regular intervals.

Fleet

To haul the blocks of a purchase apart.

Flemish Coil

Coiling a rope flat with the end in the centre and the turns lying against, without riding over each other. Not suitable where a rope has to run through a block.

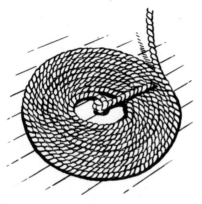

Flemish Eye

An eye formed at the end of a rope by dividing the strands and laying them over each other. Used when a soft eye is required.

Flinders Bar

A magnetic bar of soft iron mounted vertically on a binnacle, receiving its magnetism by induction from the earth. The object of the bar is to counterbalance the effect of the varying magnetism on a vessel or large yacht.

Flotation

Many classes of boats have built-in flotation—watertight air tanks filled with an expanding material to stop any leaks. Such boats will float if capsized.

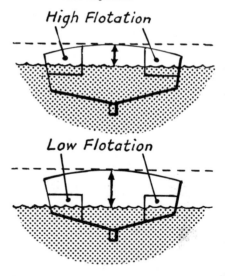

Floating Anchor

Timbers, spars, or anything that will float, lashed together and thrown overboard from the bow to lessen the drift to leeward in a gale.

Flood

The rising of flowing tide. The *floodmark* is the mark or line to which the tide rises at high-water.

Floorboards

Loose battens that cover the floors of boats to cover the bilges, and to provide a surface for walking on.

Floor Timbers

Transverse wooden members crossing the keel, and attached to lower end of frame. They tie the boat together.

Fly

(1) The horizontal measurment of a flag. (2) The compass card on which the points of the compass are marked.

Fog

Fog is merely the lower part of a cloud resting on the land or water. The usual cause is a cooling and condensing of the water droplets in the air due to the sea or land being colder than the air above it.

Fog Signals

There are rules governing fog signals. Power-driven vessels use the whistle; sailing vessels the fog-horn; and vessels being towed—the whistle or fog-horn. A power-driven vessel sounds one long blast every two minutes if under way, two long blasts if stopped. Power-driven fishing boats blow one a minute. Sailing vessels under way use a fog-horn, and blow one blast a minute on the starboard tack, two blasts on the port tack, and three blasts when running free. Vessels at anchor ring a bell once a minute.

Footrope

(1) That part of the boltrope to which the lower edge of a sail is sewn. (2) Line attached to underside of a square-sail yard to support those working aloft.

Fore-And-Aft

Not rigged with square sails attached to yards, but with sails bent to gaffs or set on stays in a fore-and-aft line.

Forecastle

(pronounced *foc'sle*). The superstructure on the forward deck, after the fore-shrouds.

Foredeck

That part of the deck in front of the bridge or foremast.

Forefoot

A piece of timber which terminates the keel at the fore-end, connecting it with the lower end of the stem. The lower end of stem where it turns off to be joined to the keel.

Fore Halyard

The rope which raises the foresail.

Fore Peak

The small space in the vessel's bows right forward. The space in the bows of a boat that is decked in.

Forereach

(1) A vessel that gains upon another when sailing close-hauled. (2) To shoot ahead, especially when going about.

Foresail

In the schooner rig it is the gaff sail on the foremast. When a sail is hanked to a forestay, it is called a forestay-sail.

Foresheets

(1) The ropes that work the foresail. (2) The forward position of a row-boat; the space beyond the first thwart.

Forestay

Part of the standard rigging, the stay running from masthead to stem.

Forward

(pronounced *forrard*). In front of, or the forepart of a vessel.

Fothering
Temporarily stopping a leak by means of a sail filled with oakum and passed under the boat into position, so that the pressure of the water forces the sail into the crack.

Foul Anchor
When a rope or cable is twisted around the anchor, or gets entangled on the sea-bed.

Four Point Bearing
A method of fixing a vessel's position when on a steady course. The four-point bearing refers to four points of the compass (a point = 11°15'), and *not* four objects on which to take a bearing. Only one object is required. Two bearings of it are taken, first when four points on the bow (45°), and again when on the beam (90°). The time is noted on each occasion and the distance run between the two bearings is the distance off the object when it is abeam. A similar method 'doubling the bow angle', may also be used for determining offshore distance.

Fox
A small rope made by hand of two or more rope-yarns twisted and rubbed backward and forward with canvas or tarred parcelling. Made in flat, round, or square form, used for seizings, sennits, gaskets, etc.

Framing
The structure of ribs, frames, etc, to which a vessel's outside planking is affixed. Frames are themselves fastened to keel and clamp as well as to stringers and floors. Frames are either bent or sawn to shape. There are three main types of framing in small craft: (1) *Transverse* framing where timbers are steam-bent, this is the conventional method. (2) *Grown* frames composed of sawn, short lengths of timber known as 'futtocks'. (3) *Laminated* frames which are made from a number of bent, thin timbers.

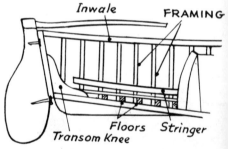

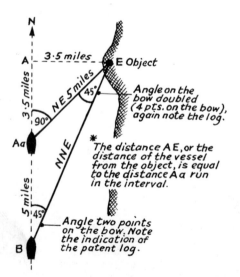

Frapping
To bind anything taut with a rope to prevent excessive movement during rough weather.

Freeboard
That part of a vessel's side above water-level to deck line or upper deck level.

French Fake
A way of coiling a rope by running it backward and forward in parallel bends, so that it may run freely.

Fuel Tank Precautions
The most dangerous combination possible is the deck plate and tank not being connected and allowing displaced fumes to settle into bilge. The only safe way is to have the tanks connected with deck plates by pipes as outlined.

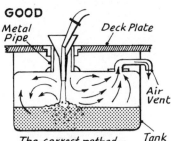

GOOD
Metal Pipe • Deck Plate • Air Vent • Tank

The correct method—tank and deck plate connected together by short pipe.

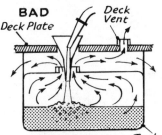

BAD
Deck Plate • Deck Vent • Tank

Fumes displaced by incoming fuel go out opening then settle in bilge.

Futtock
A section of the timbers in the built-up rib or frame of a wooden vessel, extending from the floor, half floor, or a cross-timber outward and upward to the top timber. The name also applies to the plates in a vessel's top, shrouds, and rigging, etc.

G

Gaff
The yard to which the upper edge (or 'head') of a fore-and-aft sail is attached (or 'bent').

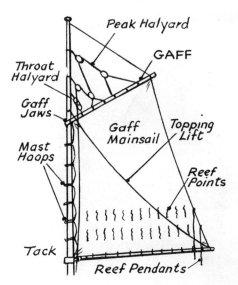

Peak Halyard • GAFF • Throat Halyard • Gaff Jaws • Gaff Mainsail • Topping Lift • Mast Hoops • Reef Points • Tack • Reef Pendants

Gaff Topsail
A light triangular sail set above a mainsail, often seen in cutters, sloops, ketches, etc.

Galley
(or kitchen). The layout of a galley should be given careful thought, as space is at a minimum. The sink, stove, ice-box, storage space for food and utensils should be planned as a whole. Attention should be given to reducing fire risk, methylated spirit is recommended for cooking as it is the only spirit that can be extinguished with water.

Gallows
One of two or more frames on deck for supporting booms, spars, etc.

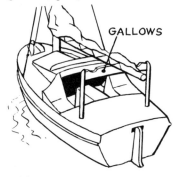

GALLOWS

Gammoning
The iron band or lashings that fasten down the bowsprit, to counteract the lifting action of the forestays.

Gantline
A rope rove through a block at the masthead for temporary use in rigging and unrigging, or for hoisting anything.

Garboards
Also known as 'garboard strakes'. The first row of planks or plates next to the keel. They fit into the keel rabbet if timber-built, and at fore and after ends on to the stem and stern deadwoods.

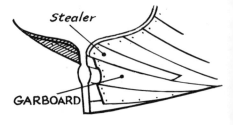

Stealer

GARBOARD

Garnet
A purchase by which the lower corner of a square sail, mainly mainsail, or foresail is hauled to the yard; a clew garnet.

Gas Detector
A vapour detector which detects the presence and accumulation of explosive gases. It is highly recommended to all boat users who have marine engines installed.

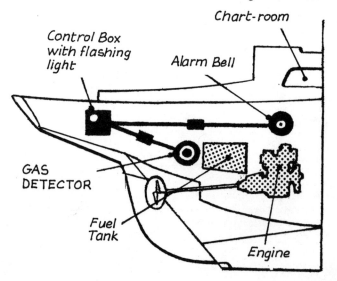

Chart-room

Control Box
with flashing
light

Alarm Bell

GAS
DETECTOR

Fuel
Tank

Engine

Gaskets
Small cords for securing furled sail to a yard, boom, or gaff.

Ghosting
A yacht under sail making headway when there is no apparent wind.

Gear
A general term for rigging and equipment; the set of ropes, blocks, etc, used in working a spar or sail.

Gimbals
The brass rings and pivots for keeping compass and chronometer horizontal when at sea.

Genoa
A large jib, used for yacht-racing. Two other types of genoa sails are used, the genoa staysail, and the masthead genoa.

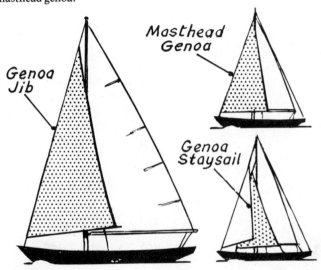

Masthead Genoa

Genoa Jib

Genoa Staysail

Getting Under Way
The process of moving off from mooring or quay side either under sail or power.

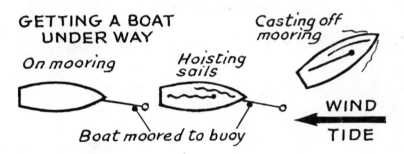

GETTING A BOAT UNDER WAY

On mooring

Hoisting sails

Casting off mooring

Boat moored to buoy

WIND

TIDE

Gin Block
A hoisting tackle block suspended from a skeleton frame, having one sheave, over which a rope runs.

Girt
A vessel moored by two cables to two oppositely-placed anchors so as to prevent swinging by wind or tide.

Give Way
To take action to prevent a collision, and to keep clear of another vessel. See also '*Rules of the Road*'.

Glass Fibre
Woven glass matting used with plastic resin for renovating old hulls or for strengthening fibre-glass hulls.

Globular Sailing
The method of sailing on the arc of a great circle, or so as to make the shortest distance between two places, A and B; circular sailing. See also *Mercator's Projection*.

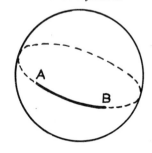

Gone By The Board
To fall or be carried overboard; as, the mast, or anything that has disappeared or got lost.

Go About
To change tack. Applied when turning with bow towards the wind.

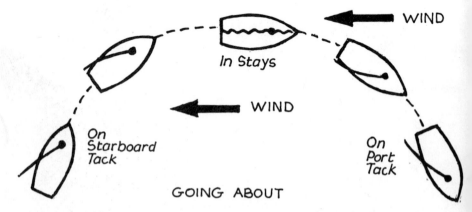

Goniometer
An instrument for measuring angles, especially the inclination of planes.

Gooseneck
The universal joint fitting at the heel of a boom to a mast, which is able to turn in any direction. Some are fitted with a pin or hook which drops into a ring attached to a mast.

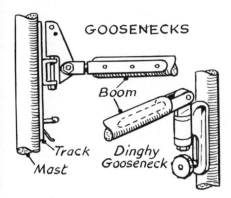

GOOSENECKS

Boom

Track

Mast

Dinghy
Gooseneck

Goosewinged
Said of a fore-and-aft rigged vessel running with headsail set on one side and mainsail on the other.

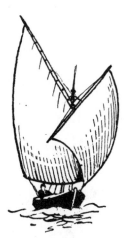

Gore
A wedge-shaped or triangular piece of sailcloth or canvas, served into a sail to give greater width or depth at a particular part.

Goring
A piece of canvas cut obliquely to widen a sail. Each piece so-cut is called a *gore*.

Graft
Weaving yarn round the tapered end of a rope, or to cover a splice, etc.

Granny Knot
A reef knot tied the wrong way; it is insecure and difficult to untie.

Grassline
(or Coir Rope). A rough rope consisting of a prepared fibre of the outer husk of the coconut; unsuitable for use in blocks and tackles, but useful for boat and rescue work. It is less strong than other ropes, but light in weight.

Great Bear, The
The constellation containing the two end stars, (Merak and Dubhe), pointing to the pole star. Used in celestial navigation.

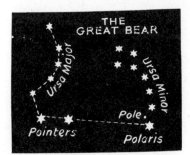

THE
GREAT BEAR

Ursa Major

Ursa Minor

Pole.

Pointers

Polaris

Greenwich Mean Time (GMT)

The system of time in which noon occurs at the moment of passage of the mean sun over the meridian of Greenwich, England. From this local time all navigational calculations are reckoned. Was established as the standard time in 1884. *Standard Time* refers to places in the same area.

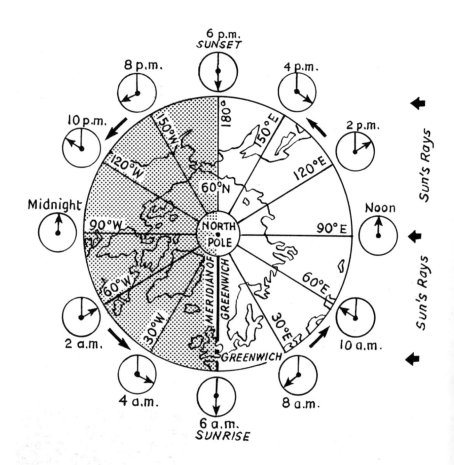

It is noon at a place when the meridian of longitude of that place passes directly under the sun.

Gripe(s)
(1) To come up into the wind in spite of the helm. (2) The curved fore-end of the keel known as the cutwater. (3) Canvas lashings for securing boats in davits.

Grommet
(pronounced *grummet*). A ring of rope made by crossing the ends of a single strand so as to form a ring, then laying or twisting those ends around the ring, usually making the circuit three times, finally tucking them in under themselves. Often used as a packing gland for sealing leaks. Also fitted around a metallic eyelet in a sail for passing lacings.

Ground Scope
The length of cable under water between two moored small-boat anchors.

Ground Swell
A broad, deep swell, caused by a long-continued gale, and felt even at a remote distance after the gale has ceased.

Ground Tackle
The tackle necessary to secure any boat or vessel at anchor, consisting of anchor, chain, warp, etc.

Guard Rails
Safety rails fitted around decks to prevent persons falling overboard. They must always be replaced after any temporary removal.

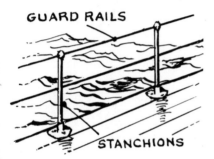

GUARD RAILS

STANCHIONS

Gudgeon
The socket attached to the stern-post to receive the pintle of the rudder. See also *Pintles.*

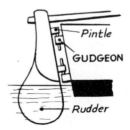

Pintle

GUDGEON

Rudder

Gulf Stream
A warm ocean current, flowing from the Gulf of Mexico northward parallel to the Atlantic coast of the United States, and turning eastward, its average rate being about 2 miles (about 3km) an hour.

Gunter
A type of mainsail, bent to a gaff that is almost perpendicular, which slides up and down the mast on rings or a strop.

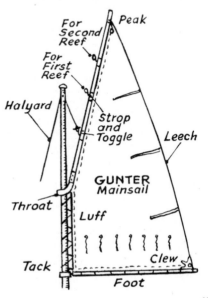

For Second Reef

For First Reef

Peak

Halyard

Strop and Toggle

Leech

GUNTER Mainsail

Throat

Luff

Tack

Clew

Foot

69

Gunter's Scale

Invented by the Revd Edmund Gunter 1588–1626, as an aid to navigation. The scale is a rule, on one side of which are marked sizes of equal parts, of chords, sines, tangents, etc, and on the other side, scales of logarithms of these various parts. By means of this scale many problems in navigation may be solved with the aid of a pair of compasses.

Gunwales

(pronounced *gunnels*). The upper edge of a vessel or boat's side, formerly used to support guns.

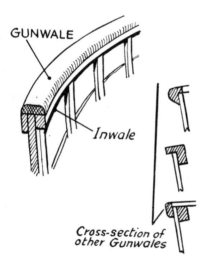

Cross-section of other Gunwales

Gut

A narrow channel of water left by the tide.

Guy

A rope used to steady or guide an object which is being hoisted or lowered. Also used to hold in place the end of a boom, spar, or yard, etc, in a sailing-boat.

Gybe

(or Jibe). Said of the boom of a fore-and-aft sail shifting suddenly from one side of a boat to the other; when the boat is steered off the wind until the sail fills on the opposite side.

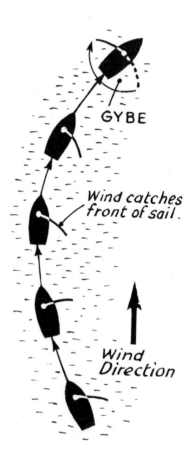

Gyro Compass

A rotating gyroscope which gives the true north when magnetic compass cannot be used. The instrument is simply a flywheel mounted on a spindle, and free to rotate and move about both the horizontal and the vertical axes. It is electrically-driven and fixed low down in the vessel.

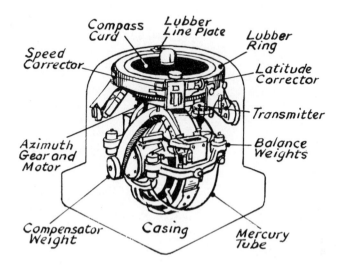

H

Hailer (Loud)

Used to give greeting or salutation to another vessel, or to arrest attention, as, to hail a person aloft, etc. The modern hailer can be used for signals, talking, or listening through.

71

Half-Mast
The position of a flag hoisted half-way up the mast, as a sign of mourning, or as a signal of distress.

Halyards
Ropes or tackle used for hoisting and lowering sails, yards, or flags, etc.

Hambroline
A small three-stranded, right-handed rope made of hemp, sometimes tarred, used for seizings, lacings, etc. An example is shown used as lashing for bitter end of anchor chain.

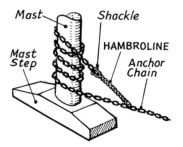

Hamper
Clumsy but necessary equipment in the way at certain times. The term also applies to spars and rigging kept aloft (top hamper).

Handicap
A factor in time and distance applied to a boat, according to her rig and design, for racing purposes.

Hand Lead and Line
A sounding-lead for shoal water, weighing 10–14lb (4.5–6.3kg) and attached to a line 25 fathoms (45.7m) in length. The lead line is marked as shown in the diagram. Used in all vessels for taking soundings by hand.

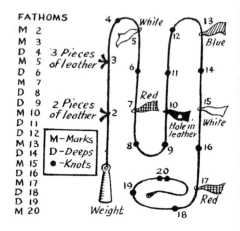

Handy Billy
A small tackle, handy for odd jobs about the deck.

Hanging Up
When tying your boat to a jetty or anchoring always allow sufficient rope for tide movements, otherwise the boat will be left hanging as the tide recedes, or will drift away on high tide through lifting the anchor from its moorings.

Hank

(1) A fitting of metal or plastic used for attaching the luff of a headsail to its stay. (2) A bundle of two or more skeins of yarn tied together.

Harpings

The foreparts of the wales surrounding the bow and fastened to the stem.

Hatch or Hatchway

An opening in the deck of a vessel which serves as a passageway or hoist way, also, a cover or door, used in closing such an opening.

Haul

(1) To pull on a single rope, '*haul away*'. (2) *Haul off*, is to sail with the wind before the beam. (3) To *haul the wind* is to turn the head of a vessel closer to the wind.

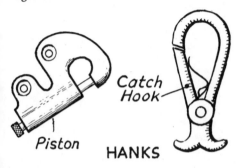

Catch Hook

Piston

HANKS

Hard A'lee

The helm put hard over to the maximum extent, away from the wind.

Hawse

(1) The area where the cables lead from a moored vessel to her anchors; also, the space between the vessel and her anchors. (2) Part of a vessel's bow where the hawseholes are.

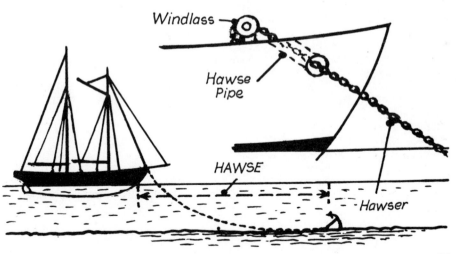

Windlass

Hawse Pipe

HAWSE

Hawser

Head

(1) The fore-end, and upper end of any object, position, or direction. (2) *Head wind*, a wind that blows in a direction opposite to the vessel's course. (3) That part of a mast between the hounds and the cap. (4) The upper edge of a square or gaff sail. (5) The bow of a vessel. (6) *Headsail*, a sail set forward of the main or foremast, a jib. (7) *Head sea*, means the sea meeting the vessel head on.

Headboard

A piece of wood used as a stiffener which is sewn in the head of a triangular sail.

Head Rope

(1) The first rope for securing a vessel. (2) That part of a boltrope which is sewn to the head of a sail.

Head Stick

A short round stick, perforated at both ends through which to thrust the head rope of a triangular sail before sewing it on; used to prevent the sail from twisting and the boltrope from kinking.

Heave

(1) Mostly used as a nautical term, as *Heave short*, to haul in cable, until the vessel is almost above the anchor. (2) *Heave a ship to*, is to bring the ship's head to the wind and stop her motion. (3) *Heave the lead*, is to take soundings with lead and line. (4) *Heave down*, is to lay a vessel on her side, when careening.

Heaving Line

A length of light rope having at one end a weighted knot which enables it to be thrown a fair distance. The other end of the line is attached to the heavy warp or hawser which should be led ashore for making fast.

Heel

(1) The afterend of a vessel's keel. (2) The lower end of a mast, spar, boom, etc. (3) The inclination of a vessel under press of canvas.

Heeling Error

A deviation of the compass caused by the heeling over of an iron vessel to one side or the other.

Helm

The tiller or wheel by which the rudder is controlled. With wheel steering, the wheel, rudder, and the head of the vessel all move to the side ordered. In boats where the helm is the tiller, the rudder and vessel's head move in the opposite direction to the tiller.

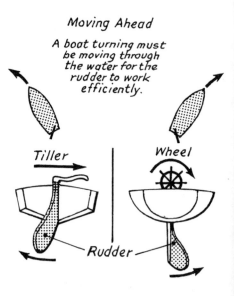

Moving Ahead

A boat turning must be moving through the water for the rudder to work efficiently.

Tiller   Wheel

Rudder

Helmsman

The man at the wheel or tiller, who steers the vessel.

Herring-boning

A form of cross-stitching used in repairing sails, to keep the seams flat.

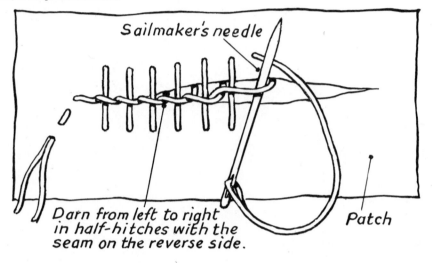

Sailmaker's needle

Darn from left to right
in half-hitches with the
seam on the reverse side.

Patch

High Seas

The open sea; that part of the ocean not in the territorial waters of any particular country.

High Water

The time at which a high tide occurs. A mark on the seashore to which the waters ordinarily reach at high water.

Hog

(1) A rough, flat scrubbing broom for scrubbing a vessel's bottom under water. (2) The flat timber secured on top of the keel; this is shaped to take the lowest plank which is the garboard strake.

Hoist

(1) To haul on a rope when a weight is being lifted. (2) The height of a fore-and-aft sail, next to the mast or stay. (3) The perpendicular measure of a flag.

Hookrope

A rope for general purposes, it is whipped one end with a hook at the other.

Plain
Hook

Reverse
Eye

Sling
Hook

Spring
Hook
for pulling
up ropes

Calliper
Hook

Hoops

Rings fitted round a mast and attached to luff of a fore-and-aft sail.

75

Horizontal Danger Angle

An angle based on the angular distance between two known visible objects given in the chart and visible at the same time. The angles in a segment of a circle are all equal. By setting this angle on a sextant or any other sighting instrument, we may keep ourselves outside (or within if desired) an unmarked danger. This method is much to be preferred to the *vertical angle.*

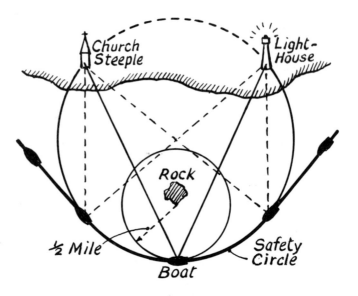

Horn Timber

Timber or timbers connected to the sternpost of a boat to form the backbone of an overhanging stern.

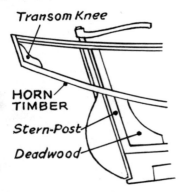

Horse

A metal rail running athwart the stern of a sailing-boat, upon which the main sheet-tackle travels.

76

Hounds Band
A band round the masthead to take the shrouds and stays.

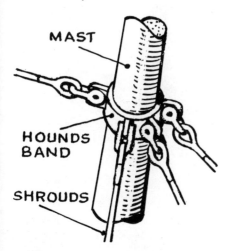

Round Bilge

Single Chine

Housing
The space below the deck of a vessel occupied by the lower end of a mast, or bowsprit.

Hove To
Lying head to wind with, in fore-and-aft vessels, staysail aback. Used when weather too rough for sailing or when you just wish to mark time. Sketch shows a yacht hove to under full sail.

Double Chine

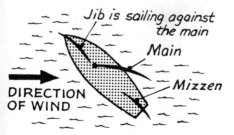

Fibre-glass Hull

HULL SHAPES

Hull
The frame and plating of a vessel, exclusive of her masts, yards, sails, and rigging.

Hydraulic Steering

A method of steering control which dispenses with levers, cables, chains, etc. For straight course steering one is able to lock the rudder.

The system consists of two working unit only; a simple multi-piston pump driven b the steering wheel, and a cylinder connecte with the rudder.

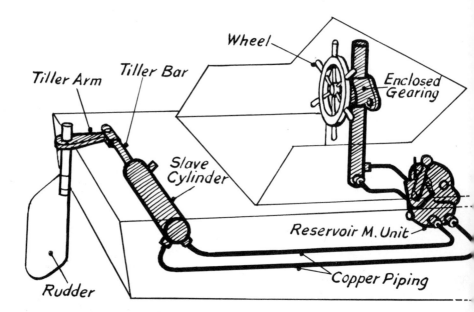

Wheel

Tiller Arm   Tiller Bar

Enclosed Gearing

Slave Cylinder

Reservoir M. Unit

Copper Piping

Rudder

Hydrodynamic Force

Relates to the pressure of water or liquids, as aerodynamic force applies to wind and sail. Hydrodynamic force applies to the force produced by water flow on hull, centreboard, and rudder. Capsizing can be due to the unbalanced weight of these two forces.

Hydrography

The science of plotting the waters and coast-lines of the world.

Hygrometer

An instrument for measuring the amount of moisture in the atmosphere. It has two thermometers, placed side by side, one wet the other dry. Readings are taken from both bulbs which give the measurement of humidity in the air.

Maximum and Minimum Thermometers

I

In Board
Within the boat, as opposed to *outboard*, the board being the side of the boat. Often applied to a motor mounted inside the boat as opposed to one mounted on the outside of the stern.

Inboard Motor
A motor within the boat, usually a four-stroke petrol motor which needs auxiliary equipment. In larger boats the diesel motor is more commonly used.

Inhaul
A rope used to draw in the jib-boom, or a traveller on a bowsprit, etc.

International Class Boats
The classes of yachts which are built to the rules of the International Yacht-racing Union, which is the world authority controlling yacht-racing.

International Code of Signals
The system of signals used between ships, yachts, aircraft, and, via short-wave radio stations, agents, etc.

Inwales
The inwales of a boat are the strakes running beneath and supporting the inner edge of the gunwale.

Irish Pennants
Frayed ends of ropes and yarns hanging about the rigging.

Isobar
A line on a weather-map connecting or marking areas of equal barometric pressure.

Isogonic Lines
Lines traced upon a chart, connecting points of equal declination.

J

Jackstay
(1) A wire rope to carry a traveller. (2) A rope used to hold a gaff topsail to its mast. (3) A rod along the upper surface of a square sail yard, to which the sail is bent.

Jackyard
A short spar to extend a topsail beyond the gaff.

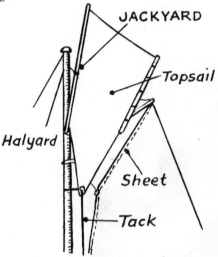

Jaw
(of a rope). The distance along a rope between two points on the same strand, ie one twist or turn of a strand.

79

Jawrope
(or parrel line). A rope partly surrounding the mast and connecting the jaws of a gaff; sometimes threaded through parrel balls, to move easily.

Jewel Block
A block at the extremity of a yard, through which the halyard of a studding sail is rove.

Jib
A triangular sail set on a stay extending from the foremast or fore-topmast head, to the bowsprit, or to the jib-boom. There are special jibs used for racing craft.

Jib-Boom
A spar or boom which serves as an extension of the bowsprit; to carry a flying jib.

Jib Header
A gaff-topsail, shaped like a jib; a jib-headed topsail.

Jib Topsail
A triangular light sail flying from the extreme forward end of the flying jib-boom, and set about half-way between the mast and the boom.

Jigger
A small tackle containing a single and double block fitted with a rope; used for various purposes; eg, to increase the purchase on a topsail sheet in hauling it home.

Jigger Mast
A mast often set at the stern of a yawl-rigged boat.

Joggle
(1) The joining of pieces of timber by means of a notched projection to prevent them from sliding. (2) *Joggle Shackle*—a long jawed shackle used in cable work.

Jumper Stays and Strut
Preventive stays, for additional security in heavy weather. The jumper stays are attached to the masthead, led over the jumper strut, and down to the mast below forming a truss, offsetting the after pull of the backstay. The jumper strut is a swept-forward spreader that gives support fore and aft as well as athwartships.

Jury Mast
A temporary mast, erected and rigged up in place of one that has been carried away.

Jury Rudder
A temporary steering arrangement, set up when the rudder is carried away or unusable.

K

Kedge
(1) A small anchor carried by yachts, for temporary anchoring or for hauling off when aground. (2) To move a vessel by hauling on alternate grounded anchors.

Kedge Reel
Used on racing and cruising yachts when in need of instant use of warps.

Keel

The keel's first function is to give the hull a grip of the water and so prevent the boat from being blown sideways by the wind, or making *leeway* as it is called. Whether or not the keel is in the form of any of those shown, the work it does is the same. A hull's stability comes from her underwater shape together with the ballast she carries; she is not solely dependent on the keel to keep her upright.

LEE-BOARDS

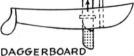

DAGGERBOARD

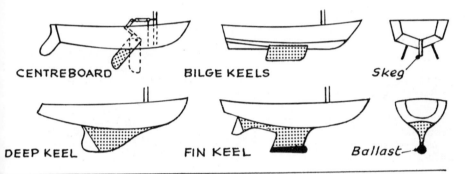

CENTREBOARD   BILGE KEELS   Skeg

DEEP KEEL   FIN KEEL   Ballast

Keelson

A fore-and-aft piece of timber fastened on top of the floors, through them to the keel, and fastened to the deadwood at each end. Generally fitted in larger types of small craft.

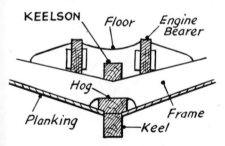

KEELSON   Floor   Engine Bearer

Hog

Planking   Frame

Keel

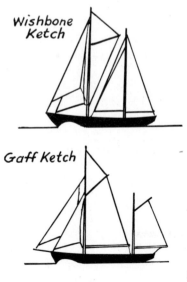

Wishbone Ketch

Gaff Ketch

Ketch

A two-masted sailing vessel rigged similarly to a yawl. A ketch differs from a yawl in having its mizzen mast stepped well before her rudder-post; the yawl has the mizzen stepped abaft the rudder-post.

81

Kicking Strap
A wire rope fitted between boom and heel of mast to keep the boom down when running before the wind.

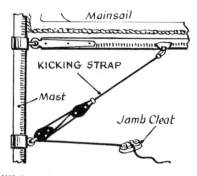

Killick
A small anchor, or heavy stone used as an anchor.

King Plank
The fore-and-aft centre plank into which sprung deck planking is nibbed.

King Post
A vertical post erected between the bottom of the hull and the deck; used as a support.

Knees
Brackets shaped from grown elbows or crooks. End supports bent to the shape of a knee, for thwarts, beams, and those connecting the transom.

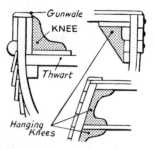

Knightheads
The heads (or chocks) fitted each side of the bow to support the bowsprit.

Knot
A measure of speed; one nautical mile per hour. (NB a nautical mile is 6,080ft or 1.15 statute or land miles; 1.85km). The term comes from the use of the old fashioned 'Chiplog'. This was a kind of drogue dropped overboard on the end of a line in which there was a knot every 25ft 4in (7.7m) (ie, 1/240 of a nautical mile). The number of knots paid out over the rail inside 15 seconds (ie, 1/240 of an hour) gave the speed of the ship in nautical miles per hour.

Knots (Rope)
A fastening together of the parts or ends of one or more cords or ropes, etc. The names of knots vary according to the manner of their making, or the use for which they are intended.

Anchor or Fisherman's Bend

Granny Knot

Blackwall Hitch

Bowline

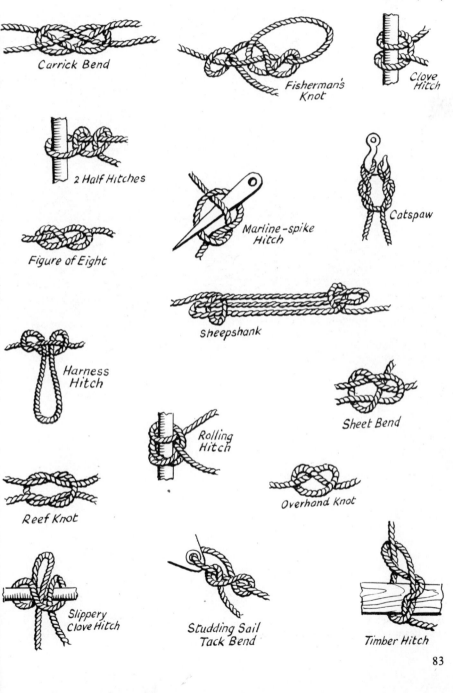

Carrick Bend

Fisherman's Knot

Clove Hitch

2 Half Hitches

Marline-spike Hitch

Catspaw

Figure of Eight

Sheepshank

Harness Hitch

Sheet Bend

Rolling Hitch

Reef Knot

Overhand Knot

Slippery Clove Hitch

Studding Sail Tack Bend

Timber Hitch

L

Lacing
A length of cord for fastening a sail or an awning to a yard, gaff, etc, or for joining two parts of a sail or awning.

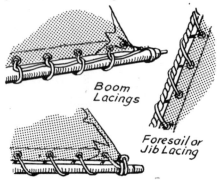

Boom Lacings

Foresail or Jib Lacing

Lamination
A method of building wooden or glass fibre parts of a boat by bending a number of layers of thin wood to any desired shape, and sticking them together with resin glue.

Landings
The overlapping of planks as in a clinker-built boat.

Lanyard
A short piece of rope for fastening to buoys and the like, especially pieces passing through the dead-eyes for making easy adjustment, and to extend shrouds, stays, etc.

Lapstrake
The method of building clinker-built boats.

Lashing
A rope for binding or making fast one thing to another.

Lasket
A loop or eye formed on the head rope of a bonnet, by which it is attached to the foot of a sail.

Lateen
A triangular sail, extended by a long yard which is slung at an angle of 45 degrees to the mast; characteristic of vessels used on the Mediterranean.

Sails designed to catch a breeze where low-level breezes are not found

Lateral Plane
The shaded area of the submerged hull, including the body of the hull, keel, and the rudder, as shown.

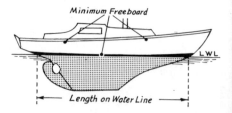

Minimum Freeboard

L W L

Length on Water Line

84

Latitude

The angular distance above or below the
equator, measured in degrees, minutes, and
seconds. See also *Longitude*.

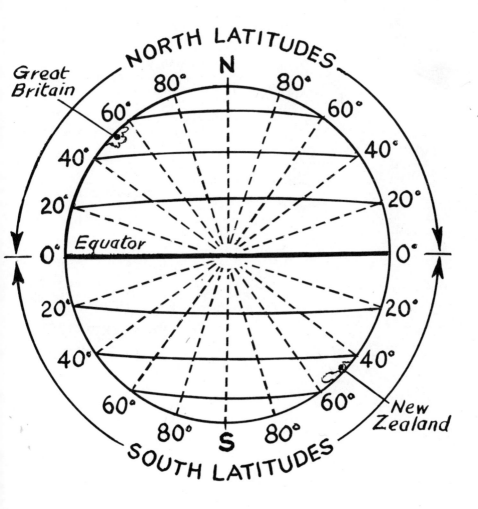

Launch

A large boat driven by motor, sail, steam, etc, usually for passengers, or pleasure trips. The name also applies to some small power-boats.

Launching

The placing of a vessel in the water. The techniques vary according to circumstances and the size of the vessel.

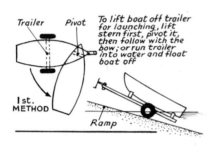

Trailer   Pivot   To lift boat off trailer for launching, lift stern first, pivot it, then follow with the bow, or run trailer into water and float boat off

1st. METHOD

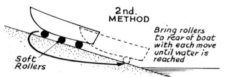

Ramp

2nd. METHOD

Bring rollers to rear of boat with each move until water is reached

Soft Rollers

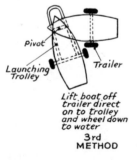

Pivot

Launching Trolley   Trailer

Lift boat off trailer direct on to trolley and wheel down to water

3rd METHOD

Lay

A sea term in common usage, eg, *lay to, lay out the cable*, or *lay a course*, etc.

Lay of a Rope

The direction in which rope strands are twisted.

Lazy Guy

A small rope or tackle by which a boom is held down to prevent it swinging about when there is no wind. 'Lazy' usually means 'extra'.

Leading Mark

A distinguishable mark on land sited to guide vessels clear of danger.

League

A distance of three miles—on land or sea—of 6,080ft (1.85km) each.

Leeboard

A board lowered on the lee side of a flat-bottomed boat, and acting like a keel or centreboard to prevent her from drifting to leeward.

LEEBOARD

Leebowing

A sailing advantage secured by taking the tide on the lee bow instead of the weather bow, in going to windward.

Leech

Either edge of a square sail; also, the after edge of a fore-and-aft sail.

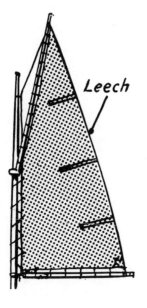

Leech Line

(1) A line leading from the edge of either side of a square sail. (2) In smaller boats, a line held loosely on the leech of mainsail or jib; to adjust the curvature of the sail. *Leech rope* that part of the boltrope to which the leech of a sail is sewn.

Lee Shore

A shore upon which the wind blows; the shore facing the lee side of a boat. (Lee means the opposite to 'weather'.)

Lee Side

The sheltered side of a vessel, away from the wind.

Leeward

(pronounced *looard*). The opposite to windward, ie, the sheltered side.

Leeway

The sideways drift of a vessel under pressure of wind; the angle between the line of a vessel's keel and that of her course.

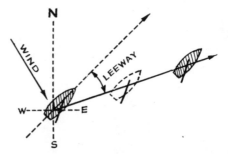

Leg

The distance run by a boat on one tack of a sailing race course between two points.

Lifebuoy

A float intended to support persons who have fallen into the water, until help arrives. To throw a lifebuoy throw it flat, and never attach a rope—you will only tow the buoy around. Use the buoy *without* a rope—to mark the spot where the man fell. This is very important at night when one uses the automatically lit type of lifebuoy.

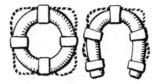

Life-Jacket

A form of buoyancy worn by sailors. It is an essential piece of safety equipment.

Liferaft

An inflatable liferaft carried by many types of vessels is stowed in a protective container, placed conveniently for launching. This type of safety equipment has separate buoyancy chambers, automatic canopy erection, sea anchor, and water-operated rescue light. There are other types more elaborately fitted out.

Lift (Topping)

(1) A rope leading from the masthead to the extremity of a yard below; used for raising or supporting the end of the yard. (2) A sudden wind shift away from the bow. See also *Topping Lift*.

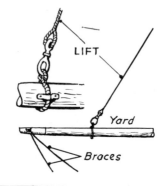

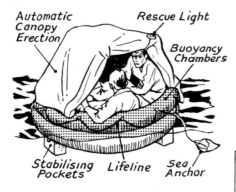

Lights at Sea

The code which relates to the lights carried by ships at sea is contained in the 32 rules listed in 'Regulations for Preventing Collisions at Sea'. The sketch shows the 2 anchor lights required by Rule 30 of the 'International Regulations for Preventing Collisions at Sea'.

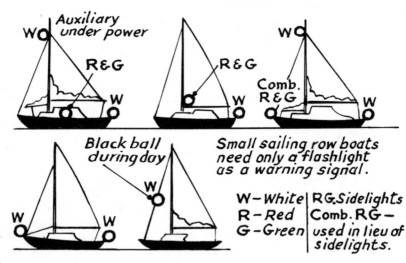

Light Vessel
A stationary vessel equipped with a brilliant light, and moored off a shoal or place of dangerous navigation as a guide for mariners.

Limbers
Holes or channel ways along each side of the keelson, for drainage to pump well.

Lines
The drawings of the shape of an intended boat, consisting of (1) the sheer plan; (2) the body plan; (3) the half-breadth plan; (4) the sail plan, usually drawn to scale or 1″ to the foot (100mm to the metre).

Loadstone
(or Lodestone). A piece of magnetic iron ore possessing polarity like a magnetic needle. It is this which enables the needle to point north.

Log-Book
The book in which the official record of a voyage is entered, such as, distance the vessel has made, log readings, the weather, or anything that has happened on board, etc.

Loggerhead
A small bollard built into a boat for securing a rope when it is running out too fast.

Lubber Line

Longitude
The distance of any place in the arc east or west measured in relation to Greenwich or any other meridian. Longitude is reckoned from 0 degrees to 180 degrees east or west. Besides being measured in degrees, the longitude is also measured in time. That is, in hours, minutes, and seconds, each hour being equal to 15 degrees. See also *Latitude*.

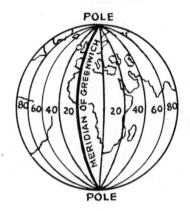

Long Jawed
Describes a rope which has stretched and become such that the strands have a tendency to untwist.

Long Splice
A useful splice, as it permits the joining of two ropes together to run through a block as easily as an unspliced rope.

Loof
That part of a vessel's side where the planking begins to curve toward bow and stern.

Loom
The end of the oar held by the oarsman.

Lubber Line
The line inside a mariner's compass bowl indicating direction in which vessel's head lies. The lubber line moves with the vessel, as she turns, while the card itself remains stationary.

89

Luff

(1) The leading edge of a sail. (2) To bring boat's head closer to the wind. (3) A purchase consisting of a double and a single block, used in various ways. When an extra luff tackle is attached to the fall of another (for increased purchase) it is termed 'luff upon luff'.

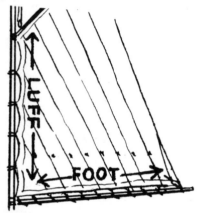

Lugger

A small beamy vessel having two masts, and carrying lug sails, usually a fishing vessel. Sometimes rigged as a gunter yawl.

Lugsail

A four-cornered sail bent to a yard that hangs obliquely to the mast, and is raised and lowered with the sail.

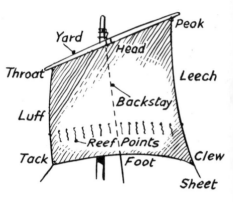

Luting

The process of making joints airtight by using putty thinned with linseed oil.

M

Magnetic Course

The angle BOS that the vessel's track makes with the magnetic meridian. This course is affected only by variation, the application of which converts it into a true course.

Magnetic Poles

The North and South in the polar regions of the earth at which the direction of the dipping needle is vertical. The North Magnetic Pole is located in the region of the intersection of the parallel of 70° north latitude with the meridian of longitude 97° west of Greenwich. The South Magnetic Pole is on the Antarctic continent, in latitude 72°25' south and Longitude 155°16' east of Greenwich.

Main Boom

The spar used for extending the foot of a fore-and-aft mainsail.

Main Brace
In square rig the purchase attached to a mainyard for setting the sail to the wind.

Main Deck
The principal deck extending the whole length of a vessel.

Mainsail
In a square-rigged vessel, a sail bent to a main-yard; in a fore-and-after the large sail is carried on the mainmast.

Main Sheet
The purchase by which the mainsail is trimmed.

Main Stay
The rope leading from the mainmast-head forward, to stay or support the mast in that direction.

Main Yard
In square rig the yard on which the mainsail is extended, supported by the mainmast.

Manilla
(Hemp). A fibrous material, obtained from the *Musa textilis*, a plant allied to the banana, growing in the Philippines. Ropes, and cables are made from its matting.

Man Overboard
The cry of alarm that should be instantly raised should any one fall overboard. In rough conditions and at night recovery of a man overboard is well nigh hopeless. Emergency drill for watch on deck after raising alarm is: (1) Throw lifebuoy in to water or preferably several, they can mark your course back to the man in the water. (2) Keep exactly on course until skipper in charge and enough crew on deck to manoeuvre ship. (3) Post lookout to keep eye constantly on man in water, (if possible). The skipper should gybe the ship round and make short tacks back along his course ending in a hove to position slightly to windward of the man in the water and drifting gently down on him. If under power, engines should be stopped until man is on board.

The point of gybing (no matter what point of sailing you were originally on) is that it puts you downwind of the man in the water (he will be drifting that way anyhow) and you will be able to tack gently up to him and to luff up instantly instead of thundering down from windward. Moreover, floating objects are more easily visible upwind than downwind.

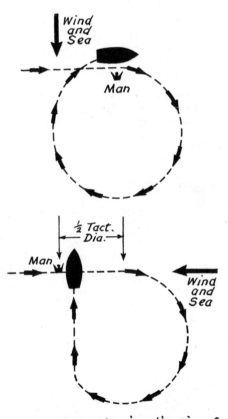

✳ 2 methods showing direction of wind before making a rescue.

Marine Engine

An engine adapted for marine use. Petrol engines are the most popular in boats up to about 35ft (10m). Diesel engines come into their own on larger craft.

Marine Speedometer

A gauge very similar to a car speedometer only the readings are in knots ranging up to 45mph (72kph) or over.

Marker Buoy

Any type of buoy such as those laid out for sailing races, etc.

Marline Spike

A pointed tool, used to separate the strands of a rope in splicing and marling. A *Marline Spike Hitch* is used for getting a leverage with a marline spike when seizing or serving.

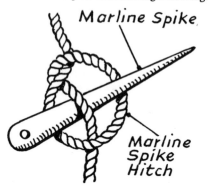

Marline Spike

Marline Spike Hitch

Marking Cable

Links marked on the cable at regular intervals so that it is known how much cable has been let out.

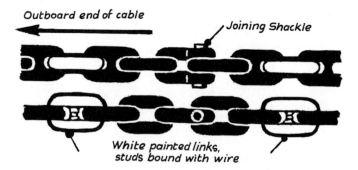

Outboard end of cable

Joining Shackle

White painted links, studs bound with wire

Marline

A small line composed of two strands a little twisted, used for winding around ropes and cables; to prevent their being weakened by fretting.

92

Marry

To place two ropes alongside of each other so that they may be grasped and hauled on at the same time. Also, to join two ropes end to end so that both will pass through a block.

Mast

The mast is a round or oval-shaped vertical pole upon which the sails are hoisted. They are in two forms: a *built-up* mast in two or three sections; and the *pole-mast* which is in one whole piece, without a topmast. *Lower Mast* is the first section of a built-up mast from the deck. Shrouds support the lower mast at a point below its top or cap.

Mast Case

The framework that keeps the mast upright to the level of the deck.

Mast Clamp

A metal loop hinged to a thwart to hold a mast in position.

Mast Coat

A piece of canvas painted or tarred and placed around a mast, where it enters the deck to keep the water out.

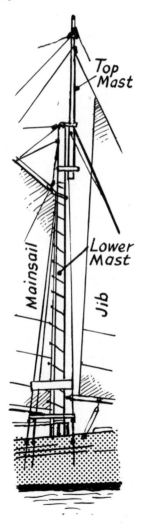

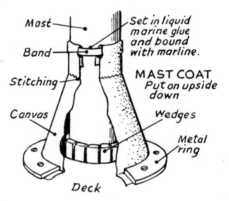

Masthead

The top of a mast where the metal fitting carrying the rigging is fixed. In small craft that portion of mast above the hounds.

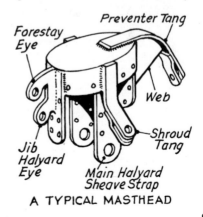

A TYPICAL MASTHEAD

93

Mast Hoops
Hoops attached to the luff of a gaff sail, which slip on the mast as the sail is raised or lowered.

Mast Partners
A strengthening frame of deck beams for supporting a mast, and relieving the deck from the strain.

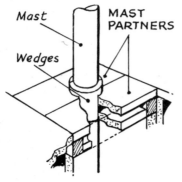

Maul
An iron or wooden hammer, used to drive the fid in or out of a top mast.

Measured Mile
A distance of one nautical mile measured between buoys, for computing a vessel's speed.

Mercator's Projection
A chart invented by French cartographer Geradus Mercator, in the sixteenth century, on which the meridians of longitude and parallels of latitude are projected in straight lines, the former parallel and equidistant the latter with the distances between them increased from the equator to each pole, so that the degrees of latitude alter proportionately. Therefore navigators always use the latitude scale to measure distance on such charts. The one small disadvantage of the Mercator chart is that a straight line on it does *not* represent the shortest distance between two points but is in fact a rhumb-line.

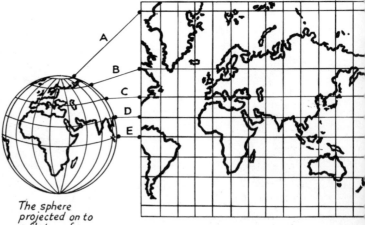

The sphere projected on to a flat surface.

Meridians

Imaginary circles round the earth at right angles to the equator, passing through the poles and zenith of any place, such as the Greenwich Meridian.

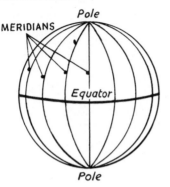

Meteorological Symbols

The meteorological elements—pressure, temperature, wind, humidity, visibility, clouds, rain, snow, or hail—are recorded at the meteorological station. The information is then sent to the forecasting stations. Each weather element is shown by a separate symbol or figure at the position of the station on the map as shown in the key diagram. See *Weather-Map*.

Metre Class

Formula boats, such as, the 6 Metres and 5.5 Metres which are built to comply with a variable formula that covers water-line length and sail area, etc.

Mile

A *nautical mile* is one sixtieth of a degree (ie, one minute) of a great circle of the earth, or 6,075ft (1851.6m).

Mizzen

The after mast or sail of a yawl, ketch, or ship. The sail is called the 'spanker' or 'driver' in full rigged ships.

Metacentre

Is the intersection of a line drawn vertically through the centre of buoyancy of a vessel in equilibrium and the vertical line passing through the centre of buoyancy when the vessel is listed. When the metacentre is above the centre of gravity, the position of the vessel is stable; when below it, unstable.

g – Centre of gravity
b – Centre of buoyancy when boat is upright
bb – Centre of buoyancy when she is listed as shown
m – Metacentre for this particular list
mg – Metacentre height
gz – Righting-lever — force of buoyancy acting upward through bb

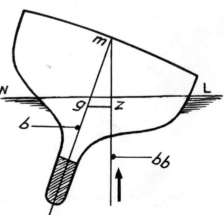

Monkey Block
A small single block strapped with a swivel, used in guiding or holding running rigging.

Monkey Seam
A seam formed in the making of a sail by laying the selvage-edges of two pieces of canvas over each other and stitching on each side and down the middle.

Mooring Hook
A hook that hooks on to any rope up to 2in (50mm) in diameter. Easily fitted to a boat-hook, or may be used alone. A safety catch is automatically released when the pole is withdrawn.

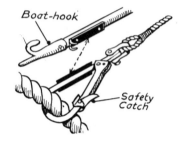

Boat-hook

Safety Catch

Mooring
Confining a vessel or boat to a particular place, by means of anchors, buoys, or warps. The art of placing a vessel midway between anchors so that she is able to ride changing tides.

* To secure a boat in a tideway two anchors are necessary to prevent drag, making sure both anchors are in line with the tide.

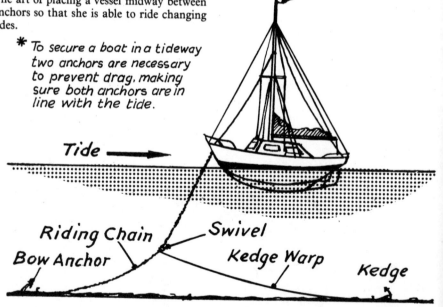

Tide ⟶

Riding Chain   Swivel

Bow Anchor   Kedge Warp   Kedge

Moorings

Any layout of anchors, weights, posts, and chains in a harbour, to which a vessel may make fast. Permanent moorings consist of a concrete clump, or two or more anchors laid opposite to each other, connected to a ground chain which, in turn, is secured to a rising chain. The rising chain is attached to the mooring buoy which can be picked up and made fast, or to which the mooring warp can be attached.

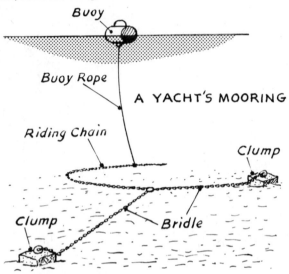

A YACHT'S MOORING

Morse Code

The signal code in which letters are represented by variations of dots and dashes, or long and short flashes; used for visual and sound signalling.

MORSE CODE AND PHONETIC ALPHABET							NUMERALS
A	·—	ABLE	N	—·	NAN	1	·————
B	—···	BAKER	O	———	OBOE	2	··———
C	—·—·	CHARLIE	P	·——·	PETER	3	···——
D	—··	DOG	Q	——·—	QUEEN	4	····—
E	·	EASY	R	·—·	ROGER	5	·····
F	··—·	FOX	S	···	SUGAR	6	—····
G	——·	GEORGE	T	—	TARE	7	——···
H	····	HOW	U	··—	UNCLE	8	———··
I	··	ITEM	V	···—	VICTOR	9	————·
J	·———	JIG	W	·——	WILLIAM	0	—————
K	—·—	KING	X	—··—	X-RAY		
L	·—··	LOVE	Y	—·——	YOKE	S·O·S	
M	——	MIKE	Z	——··	ZEBRA	···———···	

Motor Sailer

The true motor sailer can travel equally well under sail or power, the engine being more powerful than an auxiliary one. Commonly referred to as a fifty-fifty, it usually has a centre cockpit and extra roominess that power-boat owners' enjoy. Not to be confused with a sailing yacht that has a relatively small auxiliary engine or a power-boat with an auxiliary sail.

Motor

Mould Loft

A room or area on the floor of which plans of a boat are drawn up full size.

Moulds

Frames giving the true shape of a boat at a number of positions, upon which the boat is built.

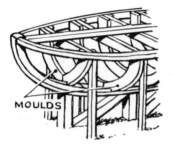

MOULDS

Mousing

A lashing of spunyarn, or wire uniting the point and shank of a hook to prevent it unhooking.

Mousing a Hook

Multihulls

Catamarans, trimarans, cathedral hulls, etc. These craft are very stable except at very high speeds, when they can capsize. The hulls vary in shape and rigging according to size. A drawback to these craft is their large beam which makes them awkward for launching, mooring, and going about.

N

Narrows

Narrow passages up a channel, river, or estuary.

Nautical Almanac

An official annual publication containing the positions of the heavenly bodies, the times of astronomical phenomena, and other data for navigational use.

Nautical Distance

The length in nautical miles of the rhumbline joining any two places on the earth's surface.

Navigation Lights

Lights carried by vessels under way to show approximately which way these vessels are heading. Vessels showing such lights are able to estimate each other's position, course, and speed, and to take action accordingly. Refer to part 'c' of 'International Regulations for Preventing Collisions at Sea' for details.

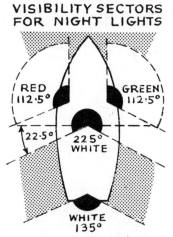

VISIBILITY SECTORS FOR NIGHT LIGHTS

RED 112·5°   GREEN 112·5°

22·5°   225° WHITE

WHITE 135°

All lights should have correct beam angle; 22·5°

Navigator

One skilled in the art of navigation whose main duty is to direct the course of a vessel.

Nettling

(1) A process by which two ropes are joined end to end so as to form one rope. (2) The tying together of the ends of yarns in pairs, to prevent tangling.

Nipping

Seizing two ropes together by a racking seizing, so that they will travel together.

Nock

The upper fore corner of a gaff-sail, or of a trysail; the throat.

Nose

The iron piece protecting the stem of an open boat, or vessel.

O

Oakum

Loose fibres obtained from picking old hemp ropes to pieces and using them for caulking the seams of vessels, stopping leaks, etc. Oakum is seldom used or seen nowadays. It has been replaced by modern products that harden quickly and have good waterproof qualities.

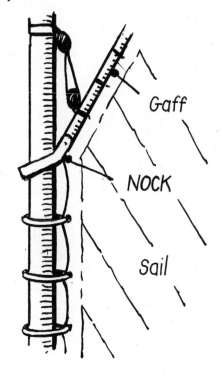

Gaff

NOCK

Sail

Oar

A pole with blade used for rowing, usually made of ash or spruce, shape depending on the type of boat.

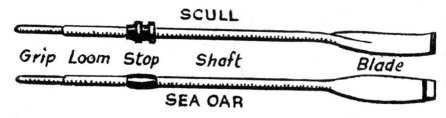

SCULL

Grip Loom Stop Shaft Blade

SEA OAR

Oarlocks

See *Rowlocks*.

Ocean

The vast expanse of sea water surrounding the earth's land surface which is divided and named in five parts: Atlantic, Pacific, Indian, Arctic and Antarctic.

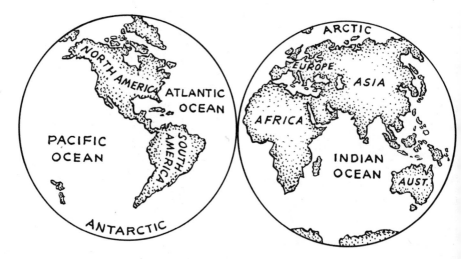

Ocean Currents

The course or direction of currents caused by the prevailing winds, and the Earth's rotation. The pattern of major currents is shown on the map opposite.

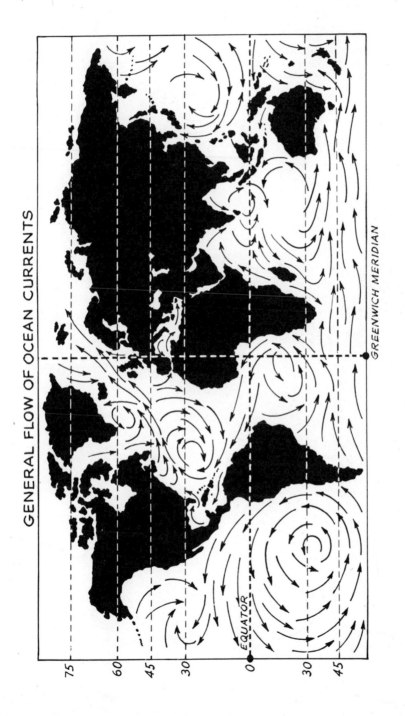

GENERAL FLOW OF OCEAN CURRENTS

Offsets Table
Detailed sections in boat-building plans done by the use of 'Tables of Offsets', giving measurements to get shapes of bow and stern-boards, etc.

One-Design Class
A class of boat with a fixed keel, they are ideal for the beginner with modest means. As the name implies, they are a group of boats which conform to a standard design.

One-Ton Cup
Originally French and goes back to 1899. Given to winners of the off-shore races; (maximum rating 22ft, 6.7m).

Outboard
The side of a vessel or anything projecting beyond the gunwale.

Outboard Motor
A propelling unit shipped over the stern of small boats; suitable for boats up to about 25ft (7.6m) in length, larger craft would require double engines. They are also used as an auxiliary on sailing boats.

Outhaul
A line used for extending the clew of a mainsail. The tack of studding sail, or hauling out the traveller on a bowsprit.

Out of Trim
(1) Said of a boat down by the head or the stern. (2) Any boat looking untidy.

Outpoint
To sail closer to the wind than another boat.

Outrigger
A spar or projection run out for temporary use, as from a vessel's mast, to hold a rope or a sail extended. Anything projecting from the side of a boat to prevent upsetting, eg, a projecting support for a rowlock on the side of a boat.

Overlap
A yacht establishes an *overlap* when overtaking the stern of the yacht being overtaken.

Overloading
Never overload your boat, if a boat is designed to be sailed with three people aboard don't go sailing with four, use common sense. It is better than struggling to keep the boat right side up.

P

Painter
The rope at the bow of a small boat, used to tie it up to anything.

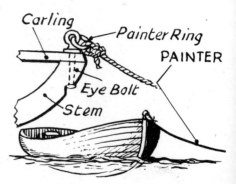

Palm

A sailmaker's leather strap with a metal pad worn on the hand, and used as a thimble to push a sail needle through canvas when sailmaking.

Parabolic Curve

The curves formed in relation to the parallels in sailmaking.

Parallel Rulers

Two rulers connected by pivoted cross-pieces that keep them parallel however they are moved. They are used for transferring a bearing or course to the nearest compass rose or *vice versa*.

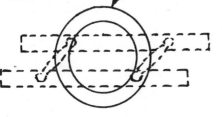

Chart Compass Rose

* To find a bearing between A and B, edge of closed parallel ruler is laid between the two places then worked over the chart to the nearest compass rose.

Parallel Sailing

Sailing along a parallel of Latitude; a safe method of navigation used before efficient methods of estimating Longitude were discovered.

Parcelling

Parcelling a rope is to cover it with strips of tarred canvas, marled down with spunyarn or twine, knotted at each turn; used for protection against chafe.

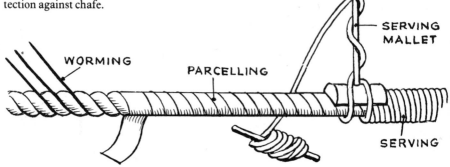

WORMING

PARCELLING

SERVING MALLET

SERVING

Parrel

A sliding loop, or rope, by which a yard is attached to a mast, so that it may be hoisted or lowered at pleasure.

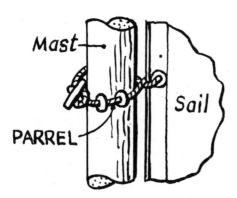

Mast

Sail

PARREL

Partners

Timber framework surrounding an opening in a deck, for the support of a mast, pump, capstan, or the like.

Pass

A sailor's term for reeving through, or to take a turn with a rope, as around a sail in furling, etc.

Patches

A tidy finish where sections of sails overlap.

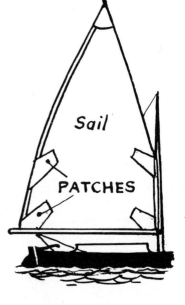

Sail

PATCHES

104

Patent Log

A mechanical device replacing the shiplog of which there are various types in use today. The log consists of a register, containing the mechanism, a dial, and a rotator which is streamed by means of a log line, the inboard end working the dial indicates the distance run through the water.

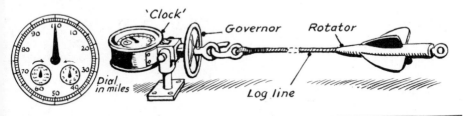

Peak

(1) The upper corner of a sail extended by a gaff. (2) The narrow part of a vessel's bow, or the part of the hold within it.

Pelorus

A pivoted metal compass that has no magnets; it is simply a compass card fitted with a movable sight; the pelorus must agree with the vessel's compass, for the sight to be accurate. Extensively used in navigation for taking bearings.

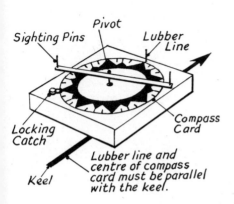

Pendant or Pennant

(1) A flag carried at the mast-head of a vessel; there are various forms. (2) A rope or strap with a thimble eye each end, to which a purchase is hooked. Used in reefing.

Perigee

The point on the moon's orbit which brings it closest to the earth and a greater tidal motion is expected. (Apogee is the opposite condition.)

Picking-up-Rope

A wire hawser having a strop and a spring hook shackled to the eye; used for securing a vessel to the ring of a mooring buoy.

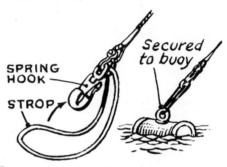

Pig Iron
Iron in oblong blocks or bars, used as ballast for sailing boats.

Pink Stern
A sailing vessel with a high, narrow stern, pointed at the end.

Pintles
Pins or hooks on which a rudder hangs and turns.

Pitch
Boiled tar used for caulking and preserving planks.

Pledge
A string of oakum used in caulking.

Plug
The wooden stopper that fits into the drain-hole of a boat, and is usually found in the plank next to the keel (called the garboard strake).

Point
One of 32 points of the compass. Each point is 11° 15' (or $\frac{1}{8}$ of a right angle) from its neighbour which is also subdivided into half and quarter points; used to indicate the general direction of the wind, or of the bearing of an object.

Plane Sailing
A term applied to the method of computing a vessel's place and course on the supposition that the earth's surface is a plane. In reality the earth is *spherical*, but for all practical purposes, is represented by straight lines on a *plane* surface. Problems relating to plane sailing may be solved in the *Traverse Tables* found in Nautical Almanacs.

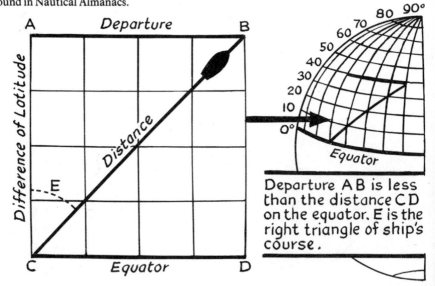

Departure A B is less than the distance C D on the equator. E is the right triangle of ship's course.

Point a Rope

To taper (a rope's end) by removing some of the yarns of each strand and bringing them to a point.

Polyester Resin

A resin for boats built in reinforced plastics. It is in the form of a clear sticky fluid and needs a catalyst added to cure (harden) it. Used to glue together layers of glass fibre matting.

Pooped

The condition of having a wave break over the poop or stern of a vessel.

Port

The left-hand of a vessel looking from stern to stem. The opposite to starboard.

Port Tack

Sailing with the wind blowing on the left-hand side of the sails.

Position Lines

Any bearings used to fix the vessel's position. In celestial navigation it consists of the measuring of altitudes and zenith distances of celestial bodies, using a sextant and the Nautical Almanac. Two sightings are required to give a 'celestial' *running fix* with the two position lines crossing at an angle.

Port Lights

(Not to be confused with portholes). Port lights are fitted to let in light and air, are watertight, with a hinged cover. In small boats, fixed portlights are called 'deadlights', and are often used in hatch tops.

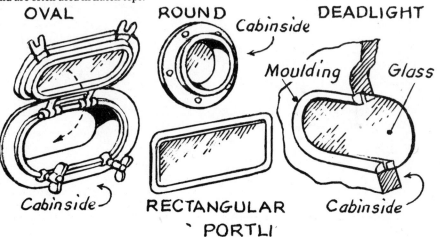

OVAL

ROUND

DEADLIGHT

Cabinside

Moulding

Glass

Cabinside

RECTANGULAR
PORTLI

Cabinside

Position Terms

The relative positions of objects outside the vessel are given in sea terms—Ahead, Astern, Abeam, which are bearings, that is, they point to definite directions. Position of an object in between these bearings is given as 'on the bow', or 'on the quarter', and so on.

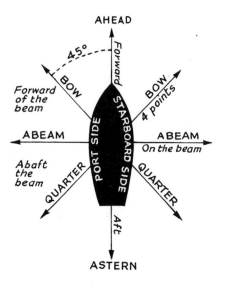

Power-Boats

These can be divided into two main groups, (a) High speed craft having very powerful engines compared with the weight of the boat. These are flat-bottomed craft which are able to plane on the surface of the water as soon as a certain speed is reached. (b) The heavier and slower 'displacement' craft of round bilge type which are driven through the water instead of over the top of it.

Pram

A flat-bottomed boat having a flat, cut-off bow instead of a sharp stem. Of Scandinavian origin. Used as a yacht's tender.

Preventers

Additional ropes to support a mast or control a boom.

Pricker

(1) A small marline spike with a wooden handle, used in sailmaking to make holes in sails. (2) A light tapering pin used in splicing small ropes.

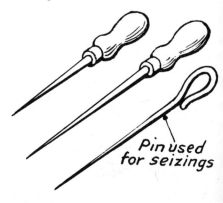

Pin used for seizings

Proa

A sailing boat with one main hull and a single outrigger. To provide stability the boat is controlled from the outrigger. It has two rudders, one at each end. To change tacks the rig is reversed and the boat steered from the other end.

Propeller
A vessel's screw: a contrivance for propelling, usually having two or more blades. In small craft it is essential for the efficiency of the engine to have fitted the right size propeller for the type of boat.

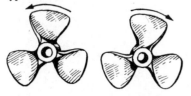

Left-hand and Right-hand Screws looking forward from rear.

Protractor
The course protractor is an instrument used for measuring angles on charts. In use, to find the bearing between two places A and B lay a straight edge or ruler between the two places; then place the protractor along the ruler with its centre C on one of the meridians, as shown in figure, and read off the bearing as indicated by the number of degrees of the arc DE reckoned from the meridian—in this case N75° W.

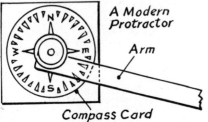

A Modern Protractor

Arm

Compass Card

✳ To find the bearing between two places, place protractor along ruler with the centre on one of the meridians, and read off the bearing from the arc d, e.

Prow
The bows and forepart about the stem of a vessel or boat.

Puddening
A lump of oakum or matting laid round the nose of a boat, to act as a permanent fender, to prevent chafing, etc.

Pulpit
A tubular structure fitted round the bow as a safety guard. The *Pushpit* is the jocular term for a similar structure at the stern end of the boat.

Purchase
A tackle, windlass, or block pulley, applied to the raising or removing of heavy objects.

Pyrotechnics
(Distress Signals). Stars, smoke, flares, or rockets; there are a variety of types and makes to suit the type and size of any boat. They should never be used for other than their proper purpose.

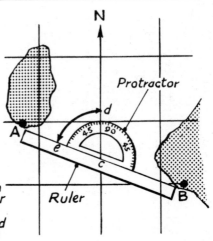

N

Protractor

d

A

e

c

B

Ruler

109

Q

Quarantine

The condition of having crew confined on board in case of suspected infectious disease in which case an all yellow flag must be displayed, so that contact between those on board and the shore is prohibited. The yellow quarantine flag is also used as a request for customs clearance.

Quarter

One quarter of a vessel, 45 degrees abaft the beam, on either side, ie, on the port or starboard side.

R

Rabbet

In boatbuilding, a stepped-shaped cut along the edge, or projecting edge of a plank to receive the edge or tongue of another plank.

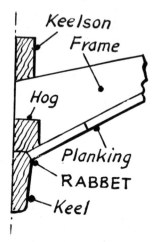

Race

A strong current of water, or the channel for such a current; sometimes produced through the meeting of two tides, or uneven sea bottom. Sketch shows how a propeller worms its way through the water creating two spiral currents which can have an effect on the operation of the rudder.

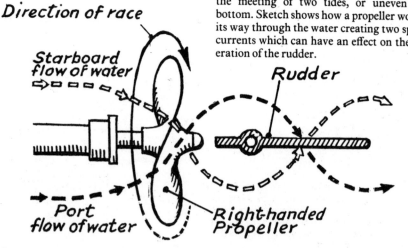

Racing

The two main forms of racing are: *Class Boat Racing*, racing on equal terms and *Handicap Racing*, that is, between boats of various types handicapped according to the first boat home, or racing on their own time or on the distance over which a race has been sailed. Races are sailed under rules a little different from the international rules observed on the high seas. These rules are strict and it is necessary to obtain a copy of them to study before tackling racing seriously.

Racing Course

A racing course can be a variety of shapes, the triangular course being the most popular. This course gives competitors a leg on each point of sailing—a beat, a reach, and a run. All three marks are passed on the same side.

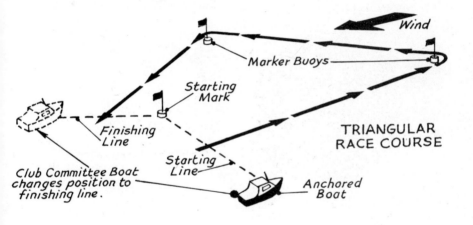

Rack

To seize two ropes together to prevent them from running out of the blocks, by putting the seizing on, over, and under each part in a figure-of-eight and covering with a few turns.

Radar

(Radio Direction and Range). An aid to navigation during poor visibility, it is similar in principle to the echo-sounder. A wave is transmitted and its echo is received and measured. The range of the object is indicated to scale on a cathode tube; the aerial (or scanner) is kept rotating to enable relative bearings to be obtained. All objects in the vicinity of the vessel are displayed on a screen with the observer vessel in the centre. The screen is called the Plan Position Indicator.

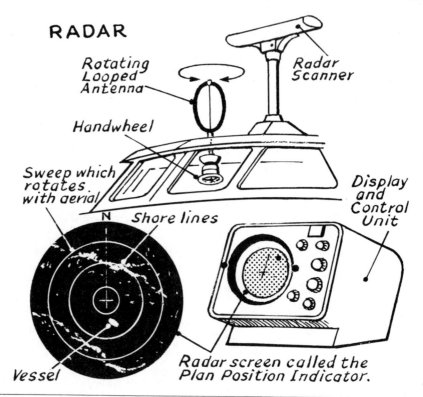

RADAR

Rotating Looped Antenna

Radar Scanner

Handwheel

Sweep which rotates with aerial

Display and Control Unit

N

Shore lines

Vessel

Radar screen called the Plan Position Indicator.

Radar Reflector

A device fitted on vessels and attached to buoys and shore stations; used as a position indicator which reflects a radar beam giving the position of these objects, moving or stationary, in darkness or fog.

Radio Beacon

An apparatus that sends out signals continuously and can be picked up by vessels equipped with a Radio Direction Finding apparatus; these are available for all types of yachts.

Radio Direction Finder

A radio aid to navigation, the apparatus supplies two or more bearings of RDF stations and once these are obtained, can be plotted on the chart. It is operated by means of a handwheel fitted to the lower end of a vertical spindle which extends down through the deck to the chartroom below. The loop aerial above picks up the radio waves and the oncoming signal is received from the transmitting station.

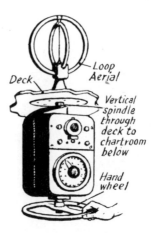

Radio Telephone

The short-range telephone service for keeping in touch with other vessels and subscribers ashore. A fitting arrangement is shown in the sketch. For the apparatus to function properly it is necessary to install a suppressor, to check interference from electrical equipment on the boat.

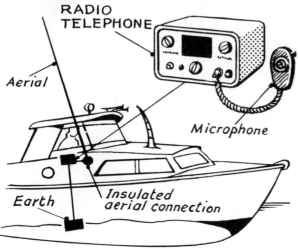

Raffee Sail
A triangular sail set above a squaresail in a fore-and-aft rigged ship.

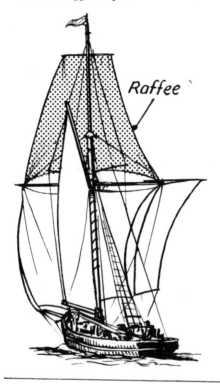

Rake
The forward or backward inclination of a vessel's bow, stern, masts.

Rating
The class of vessel or boat for marine insurance, determined by its relative safety as a risk.

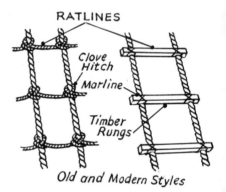

RATLINES

Clove Hitch

Marline

Timber Rungs

Old and Modern Styles

Ratlines
The small ropes fastened across the main shrouds to resemble a ladder, for going aloft.

Reach
The distance between two bends in a river, there may be an upper or lower reach.

Rain Gauge
An instrument for measuring rainfall at a given place or during a given time. 1in (25mm) of rain caught in the rain gauge represents a rainfall at 107 tons per acre.

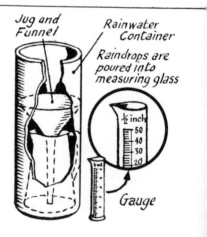

Jug and Funnel

Rainwater Container

Raindrops are poured into measuring glass

½ inch

50
40
30
20

Gauge

Reaching

Sailing across the wind. There are three types of reach: *close reach* when wind is forward of the beam; *beam reach* when wind is on the beam; and *broad reach* when wind is abaft the beam.

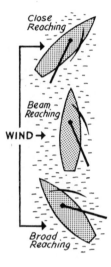

Reaming Iron

An instrument used by caulkers, for opening seams or widening holes to take the oakum.

Reef

That part of a sail which is taken in or let out by means of the reef points in order to adapt the size of the sail to the force of the wind.

Reef Bands

Pieces of canvas sewn across a sail to strengthen it in the part where the eyelet holes for reefing are made.

Reef Cringles

Thimbles sewn or spliced into leech and luff of sails through which reef pendants are rove.

Reef Earings

(Reef Pendants). Short pieces of rope rove through the reef-cringles, by which the tack and clew of the sail are secured to the yard or boom in reefing.

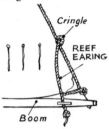

Reefing

The process of shortening sail. In yachts with their fore-and-aft rig two methods are used: (1) The traditional points reefing system whereby, as the halyard is slackened off, the tack and clew cringles are hauled down to the boom by means of the reef pendants and the foot of the sail furled and tied with reef points. (2) The patent roller reefing gear where, by means of the worm and pinion gear at the gooseneck, the boom can be rotated as the halyard is eased off thus taking up the excess sail on the roller blind principle. With square sails, the reef cringles are hauled up to the yard.

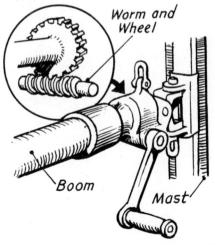

115

Reef Point
One of a series of small ropes used for securing the reefed portion of a sail.

Reef Tackle
A tackle by which the reef cringles of a sail are hauled up to the yard or down to the boom for reefing.

Reeve
The nautical term, meaning to pass, or run a rope through a block or eyelet.

Relieving Tackle
Tackles that may be attached to a tiller for assisting the steering in bad weather, or in a case of accident. Also, a tackle used to ease and help to right a listed vessel, as by attachment to a wharf.

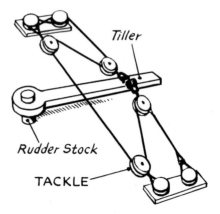

Remote Lever Control
A popular and simple control method is the easy to operate type in the single action lever, which operates both gears and throttle. Gear lever *must* be in *neutral* position before using handstart.

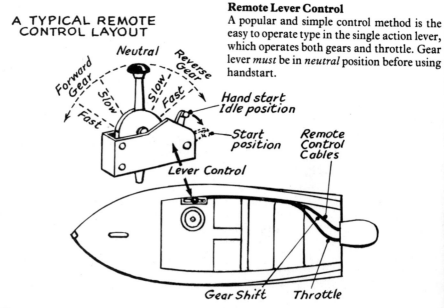

Remote Steering
A system of pulleys and cables in the steering on runabouts or similar craft.

Render
To give, to yield, to operate freely.

Rhumb-Line
In navigation, the course, or track of a vessel which intersects all meridians at the same angle: in other words, the angles a1, a2, a3, etc, are all equal. Since the meridians all converge toward the pole, this line, called the Rhumb-line, in its continuity is an unending spiral always approaching the pole but never actually reaching it. The reason for this is that the pole, bearing due north, cannot be reached on any other course than due north.

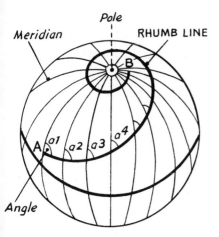

Ride
To be anchored without dragging. A ship rides to her anchor.

Rig
The arrangement of sails, rigging, masts, etc, on a vessel or boat: frequently combined with the name of a particular style of craft; as, a schooner-rig, sloop-rig, yacht-rig, etc. There are two rigs, viz, *square-rig*, a rig in which the sails are bent to the yards that lie across the masts horizontally, and the *fore-and-aft* rig in which the sails are bent on booms, gaffs, and stays, lengthwise on a vessel, as in a sloop or schooner.

Rigging
The term used for all the ropes and wires which support masts, yards, and sails.

Rigging Screw
A small bottle-screw clamp for adjusting stays or shrouds. Sometimes called a turn-buckle or, more often, a bottlescrew.

Ringtail
A narrow strip of sail set abaft and beyond the leech of a boom and gaff sail.

Rising(s)
(1) In shipbuilding, the dead-rise of a vessel's framing. (2) A narrow strake secured to the inside of the frames to support the thwarts of a boat. (3) A timber or timbers worked into the floor-seat and keel to stiffen the floor timbers where there is considerable rise. (4) A curved line showing on the drafts of a vessel, the height of the floor timbers all the way along above the keel.

Roach
(1) The convex curve or arch in the foot of a square sail, so cut as to clear the fore-and-aft stay of the mast next below. (2) The curved leech of a fore-and-aft sail; to keep the roach in shape 'battens' are used to stop flapping.

Roads
A place where vessels may shelter, and ride at anchor at some distance from the shore.

Robands
Small lines rove through eyelets in head of a square or gaff sail to lace it to the yard or gaff.

Rockered

A rounded keel, shaped like a rocker, usually seen in small boats or racing yachts.

Rolling

The transverse motion on a vessel. Rolling is caused by a beam sea, that is, with the wind abeam, and heeling alternately from side to side. The vessel rights itself by using the weights disposed in her hull in leverage with the buoyancy of her hull.

Rope

General nautical term for all cordage over 1in (25mm) in circumference made by twisting strands of hemp, manilla, coir, sisal, etc, into one. There are three main types of rope: hawser, cable, and shrouds. Today much use is made of synthetic fibre ropes, such as, nylon and terylene, which are much stronger than fibre ropes.

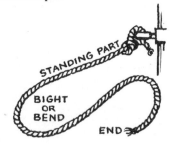

Rope Coiling

Right-handed rope must be coiled down clockwise, and left-handed rope must be coiled down anti-clockwise.

LEFT-HANDED   RIGHT-HANDED

RIGHT-HANDED ROPE COILED CLOCKWISE

Roping Needle

A large needle with its point curved, used with twine for roping sails.

Round the Buoys

A sailing term used in day racing on a closed course starting and finishing at the same place.

Round Turn

One turn of a rope round a timber; a belaying pin, etc, used to check its motion.

Rowlocks

Square notches in gunwale of a boat which act as a purchase for oars. Now universally (if inaccurately) used for crutches.

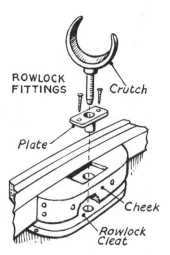

ROWLOCK
FITTINGS

Crutch

Plate

Cheek

Rowlock
Cleat

Rubber

A small iron instrument used to rub or flatten down the seams of a sail.

Rubbing Strake

A strip of wood along the outside of a boat, used as a protective buffer.

Rudder

The broad flat board of varying forms that is hinged vertically to the stern-post of a vessel, or at the stern of a boat, by which it is steered.

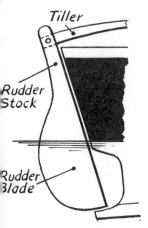

Tiller

Rudder
Stock

Rudder
Blade

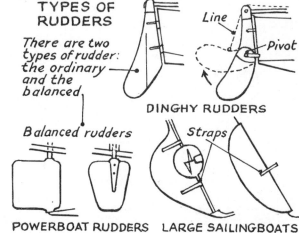

TYPES OF
RUDDERS

There are two
types of rudder:
the ordinary
and the
balanced

Line

Pivot

DINGHY RUDDERS

Balanced rudders

Straps

POWERBOAT RUDDERS   LARGE SAILINGBOATS

119

Rudder Chains

Two chains, one fitted each side of the rudder to control it, in case the rudder head should be damaged, and to prevent loss in heavy seas.

Running

Boat sailing with or in same direction as the wind with sails slackened out. To avoid a gybe, a zigzag course downwind or gybe tacking is much safer.

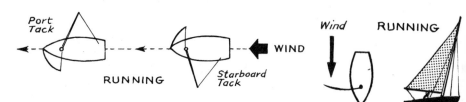

'Rules of the Road'

('The Regulations for Preventing Collisions at Sea'). A code that has been adopted by all nations who use the high seas; aspiring seamen should read and understand them. It is divided into parts as follows:

Part A General   Rules 1–3
Part B Steering & sailing rules Rules 4–19
Part C Lights & shapes   Rules 20–31
Part D Sound & light signals   Rules 32–37
Part E Exemption   Rule 38
Annex I Positioning & Technical details of Lights and Shapes
Annex II Additional Signals for Fishing Vessels fishing in close proximity.
Annex III Technical Details of Sound Signal Appliances.
Annex IV Distress Signals.

Run

(1) The aft part of a vessel's bottom where the lines converge from the floor timbers to the stern-post. (2) To sail before the wind, as distinguished from close-hauled. (3) The distance covered by a vessel.

Runners

Lines or backstays that support the mast, running from a point on the after side of the mast, to just abaft the cockpit, on either side, which can be hauled upon when required. They are usually set up either by winches or levers.

Running Fix

A method of fixing a vessel's position on a chart by means of two bearings of the same object. The second bearing being taken after a lapse of time during which course is carefully maintained and distance run noted. This will enable the vessel's position to be plotted, as shown in the sketch.

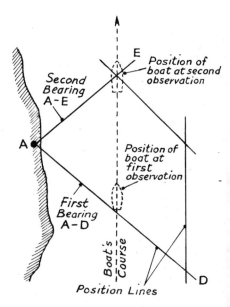

Running Free

Sailing with the wind blowing from astern.

Running Rigging

That part of a vessel's rigging that passes through blocks, used for trimming and controlling the sails—as distinct from *standing rigging*.

S

Safety Equipment

All who take up boating should carry the proper safety equipment for use in an emergency. The type of equipment carried depends on the type of boat, and for what purpose she will be used. Most countries have strict rules as to number of lifebuoys and size of liferaft to be carried, etc.

Sailing Angle

A boat cannot sail directly against the wind, it can sail no closer than an angle of 45 degrees, as it will cause the sail to luff, which means the wind strikes the lee side of the sail causing the sail to flutter.

Sailing Free

Sailing with the wind abaft the beam; able to move to either side of the course steered; not to be confused with 'running free'.

Sailing Terms

In learning to sail one not only needs a boat but should also be careful to use correctly the terms needed in sailing. Some of the more important are given here:
Locations in a boat:
For'ard, aft, amidships, in the waist, foresheets, sternsheets, to windward, to leeward.
Parts of a mast:
Head, hounds, partners, heel.
Sides of a sail:
Head, foot, luff, leech.
Corners of a sail:
Peak, throat, tack, clew. (In a triangular sail the top corner is the head.) Sails are roped on the port side.

Other spars are:
Bowsprit (in the bows), boomkin (on the stern), gaff (with jaws), yard (without jaws).
Sails are:
Jib, staysail, mainsail and mizzen. Jibs and staysails carried before the mainmast are referred to as headsails. In schooner-rig the sail on the foremast is called the foresail.

Sailmaker's Bench

The sailmaker's stock-in-trade; the bench is made so that a person at work can slide along as the job progresses, with the necessary tools at hand.

Sailmaker's Tools

Not many tools are required for making a sail. For a light sail such as the smaller lugsail type all that is needed is a batten, or spline, for marking off the rounds (parabolic curves), a pair of scissors or knife (sailcloth must never be torn), a sewing machine, a rule, a strong needle, and ordinary splicing gear.

Sail Markings

Nearly every class of racing yacht has a letter or insignia on the mainsail signifying the class to which she belongs, and her number below.

Sail Plan

A diagram showing a boat's rig and measurements, etc.

Sails

The assemblage of cloths designed to catch the wind and propel a vessel. They are of two kinds; square sails, and fore-and-aft sails. The cotton sailcloth used in former years has now been almost superseded by dacron. Where cotton sailcloth stretched under strain, shrank when wet, and was subject to mildew and rot, dacron has none of these problems. Its fibres are water-repellent and it is not affected by humidity. Nylon is also used because of its elasticity.

Sails: Cut of Cloth

The choice of cut depends on the type of boat, and what best suits it. If in doubt, it is best to have foresails mitre-cut, so that cloths run at right angles to both foot and leech, meeting on a centre seam; also, best for loose-footed mainsails. Vertical-cut is considered best for gaff mainsails, where leech is required to take the strain between ends of gaff and boom. Cross or horizontal-cut is suited to bermudian mainsails, with the cloths striking the leech at a right-angle. A foresail can be scotch-cut where the last seam bisects clew, and cloths lie parallel to leech and foot; mainly used for cheapness.

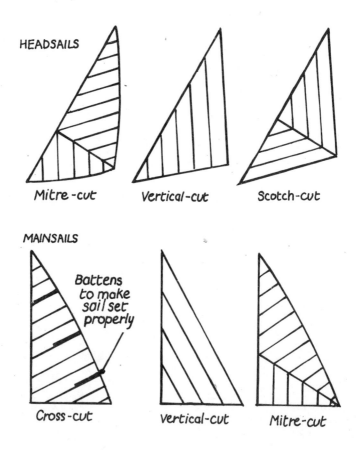

HEADSAILS

Mitre-cut   Vertical-cut   Scotch-cut

MAINSAILS

Battens to make sail set properly

Cross-cut   Vertical-cut   Mitre-cut

Salutes

Are marks of respect. They can be the discharge of guns or the use of flags by ships, or dipping the flag once only and hoisting it when the salute has been answered. Salutes should never be given by the whistle or horn.

Samson Post

A strong pillar passing between decks and resting on the keelson, supporting the beam of a deck. Some sea-going yachts have a samson post on the forepart of the deck, for taking any towing or anchoring strain.

SAMSON POST

Keelson

Scandalize

To trice up the tack and drop the head of a peak to reduce sail area. Done in square-rigged vessels to the spanker or mizzen, in a fore-and-aft rigged vessel to the mainsail.

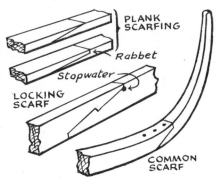

PLANK SCARFING

Rabbet

Stopwater

LOCKING SCARF

COMMON SCARF

Scarfing

In boatbuilding, the joining together of two pieces of wood, by thinning off the ends of each and overlapping them.

Scend

The lift of a boat to meet the waves, distinct from pitching, when bow and stern rise and fall alternately.

Schooner

A fore-and-aft-rigged vessel with two or more masts, usually named by its rig, eg, topsail schooner, staysail schooner, etc. In a two-masted schooner the mainsail is the larger aftermost sail.

Scotchman

A protection of wood or metal placed over shrouds and other rigging to prevent chafing by running gear.

Scow

A flat-bottomed sailing boat with square ends and twin rudders. Not suitable for open waters. Mostly of open class design.

Screw Eye-Bolts

Bolts that screw into the deck or elsewhere, as rope guides; frequently used in sailing boats.

Screw Race

The thrust of two spiral currents created by the turning of the screw. The rotating water is driven astern by the thrust imparted to it by the after side of the blades when the engine is going ahead.

Scudding

To be driven swiftly, or to run, before a gale, with little or no sail spread. The masts, yards, rigging, etc of a vessel being sufficient to give her way. The noun, scud, means cloud, spray or foam blown off the sea surface by high winds. When it appears most yachtsmen decide to make for shelter in the nearest port.

Sculling

Propelling or steering a boat with a pair of sculls, or with a single scull or oar worked over the stern obliquely from side to side. The scull is a short oar with a curved blade used by a single rower.

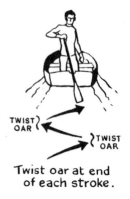

TWIST OAR

TWIST OAR

Twist oar at end
of each stroke.

Sea Anchor

It is simply a cone-shaped canvas bag attached to a line which is allowed to drift ahead of a boat in rough weather, enabling her to keep head to wind and sea and lessening her drift away from the wind. Size of the cone depends on the length of the boat. Some spars and timbers lashed together are effective as a floating anchor.

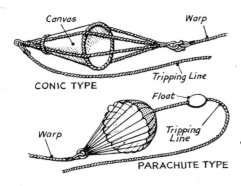

Canvas   Warp

Tripping Line

CONIC TYPE

Float

Warp   Tripping Line

PARACHUTE TYPE

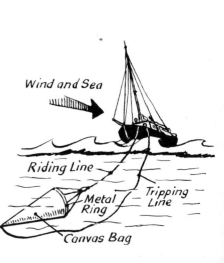

Wind and Sea

Riding Line

Tripping Line

Metal Ring

Canvas Bag

Scuppers

Drain holes in the bulwarks which allow water to escape overboard from the deck.

Sea

A large wave, ie the expression 'the vessel shipped a *sea*'.

Sea Fog

A fog that forms when air blows from warm sea to cold sea. Fog differs from cloud only in being near the ground or sea.

eizing

he operation of securing two parts of a rope
•gether with small rope or yarn. There are
aree types of seizing—*round seizing*, *flat
•izing*, and *racking seizing*.

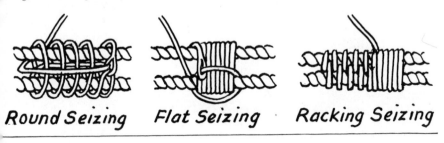

Round Seizing　**Flat Seizing**　**Racking Seizing**

elf Steering Gear

, boat steered by means of a wind vane, and
narrow rudder swinging from the main
udder. The gear consists of a plywood vane
eely pivoted on a spigot, able to revolve
1rough 360° in the horizontal plane. It can
e locked in any angular position relative to a
eaching arm with its pivot. The arm carries
pin which can be locked in any position so
1at the vane can be adjusted over the
udder. In operation, the vane is locked rela-
.ve to the arm so that it lies with the appar-
nt wind on the desired course when the
udder is amidships. If the boat luffs the vane
•ill swing towards the fore-and-aft position,
cinging the helm up, and the boat away
ack on her course, the vane centring the
elm as course is required.

elvagee

, skein of rope yarns wound round with mar-
ne, used for stoppers, straps, etc, such as,
•r lifting or moving a spar.

emaphore

, method of signalling with arms and flags.

erve

'o wind spunyarn, or the like, tightly around
rope or cable, so as to protect it from chaf-
1g or from the weather.

Serving Mallet

A wooden instrument shaped like half of a
hollow cylinder, and provided with a handle,
resembling a mallet, used in serving ropes,
cables, etc.

Set Flying

Said of a jib or staysail not hanked to a stray
but supported only by its halyard.

125

Sextant

An instrument for measuring the angular distance between two objects, and between a heavenly body and the horizon, by a double reflection from two mirrors: used especiall in determining latitude at sea by taking th sun's altitude at noon.

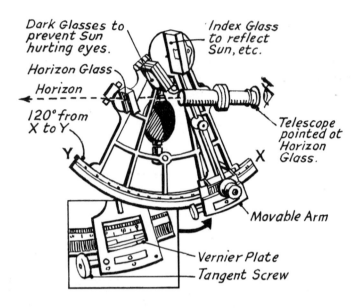

Dark Glasses to prevent Sun hurting eyes.

Horizon Glass

Horizon

120° from X to Y

Index Glass to reflect Sun, etc.

Telescope pointed at Horizon Glass.

Movable Arm

Vernier Plate
Tangent Screw

Shackle

A U-shaped metal link, fitted with a movable bolt: there are various types for a number of uses, such as, for connecting chains, lengths of chain, cable, or the like.

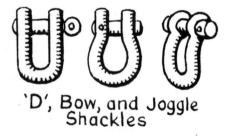

'D', Bow, and Joggle Shackles

Shake

A longitudinal split along the grain in mast and spars.

Sharpie

Applicable to keel-less boats; this narrow carvel, shallow, hard chine boat has a rock ered bottom, that is, a bottom bent upward at the bow and stern, is fully decked excep for a narrow cockpit and carries gunte mainsail, and large jib.

Sheave

The grooved wheel in a block.

Sheer

(1) The upward curvature of the deck, gun wale, and lines of a vessel, as when viewe from the side. (2) To deviate from a course.

Sheer Legs

Two or more heavy poles attached near the top and spread-eagled at the base, to form a sort of crane, and furnished with a hoisting tackle. Used for stepping the mast of vessels, yachts, or putting in the engine, etc. Also used in dockyards.

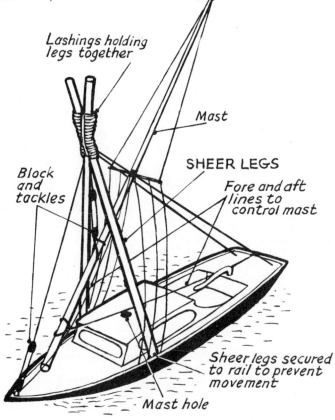

Lashings holding legs together

Mast

SHEER LEGS

Block and tackles

Fore and aft lines to control mast

Sheer legs secured to rail to prevent movement

Mast hole

Sheer Plan

The longitudinal sectional and vertical plan, fore-and-aft in boatbuilding. A normal sheer plan slopes down from the stem to about amidships and then rises towards the stern.

Sheer Plank

The deck plank nearest to the side of the vessel, usually overlaps the sheer strake.

Sheer Strake

The strake under the gunwale on the top side.

Sheets

Ropes attached to the clew of a sail and which control its angle to the wind. The expressions, 'foresheets' and 'sternsheets' merely refer to the clear space in the bows and stern of a small boat.

127

Shelf

A horizontal strip of timber extending along the inside of the frames of a yacht's hull, to stiffen it and support the deck.

Shifting Backstay

A temporary stay that has to be let go whenever the boat tacks or jibes.

Shrouds

Wire ropes serving as side stays to support the masts. There are two sets of shrouds, upper and lower. The upper shrouds support the upper part of the mast, and pass over the ends of the spreaders.

Side Lights

The red (port) and green (starboard) navigation lights carried by sailing vessels. These are placed so as to show from right ahead to two points ($22\frac{1}{2}°$) abaft the beam on their respective sides. Smaller vessels may carry a combined red and green lantern instead of having them fixed separately.

Signal Gun

Or pistol, specifically used for starting a boat race, or firing a distress signal.

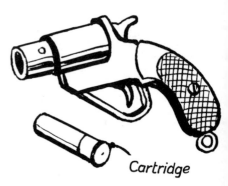

Cartridge

Signal Halyard

The halyard used for sending signal flags up to the spreader.

Signalling Mirror

A hand mirror used as a safety measure for daytime signalling in sunlight.

Sinker

A weight attached to a sounding line or a fishing line. Also, a weight used with a buoy-rope.

Sit Out

Leaning out over a gunwale or side of deck to retain balance in a dinghy or boat.

Skin

The outside planking or plating which covers the ribs of a vessel.

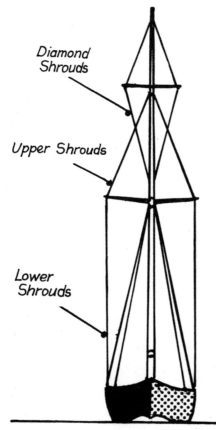

Diamond Shrouds

Upper Shrouds

Lower Shrouds

keg

he timbers used to deepen the afterpart of a
eel. A metal or wood extension of the keel, to
hich the rudder is attached.

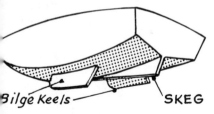

Bilge Keels — SKEG

lack Water

, brief period at high and low water when
ie tidal stream is stationary.

latting

'he violent shaking or flapping of a sail
vhen being hauled down.

lip Rope

, rope with both ends on board so that cast-
ng loose either end frees vessel from her
noorings. cf, the expression, 'let slip'.

loop

, small, one-masted, fore-and-aft rigged
essel with mainsail and jib. The *masthead
loop* has the canvas set forward of the mast
n the stay leading from the deck to the head
f the mast, whereas in the ordinary sloop it
s set lower down. The bowsprit is now
almost obsolescent.

Snotter

The short chain or rope with an eye spliced in
each end, supporting the heel of the sprit in
spritsail rig.

Mast

Sprit

SNOTTER

Gunter
Sloop

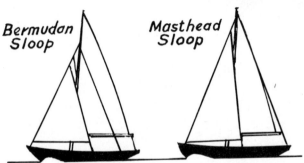

Bermudan
Sloop

Masthead
Sloop

Snub
To check a cable or rope suddenly in running out. To bring up hard on the anchor.

Sny
(1) An upward bend in a piece of timber; the sheer of a vessel. (2) A toggle attached to a flag.

SNYING
Curved planks
placed edgewise.

Sole
(1) A timber or iron piece fitted on the lower edge of a rudder, to make it even with the false keel. (2) A cabin deck. (3) A foundation plate for a marine engine.

Span
A rope having its ends made fast so that a purchase can be hooked to the bight. Also, a rope made fast in the centre so that both ends can be used.

Spanish Reef
A figure-of-eight knot tied in the head of a jib-headed sail to reduce its size.

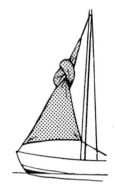

Spanker
The gaff sail on the mizzen of a full-rigged ship, sometimes called a *driver*.

Spars
A general term for masts, yards, booms, gaffs, etc.

Spherical Triangle
A Celestial Navigation method of obtaining longitude by drawing a triangle on the surface of a sphere and its arcs of great circles, its lengths being measured in degrees, minutes, and seconds (or in miles, as, 1' on a great circle = 1 nautical mile). An example is the triangle with its three corners PXZ.

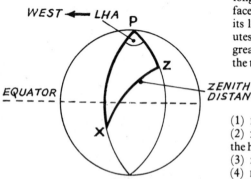

(1) P, the North Pole.
(2) X, the observed geographical position of the heavenly body.
(3) Z, Observer's position.
(4) LHA, Local Hour Angle, always observed and measured in a westerly direction.

Spider Band
An iron band round a mast, or spar, fitted with eyes to take the shackles of shrouds, etc. It may also carry belaying pins for the running gear.

Spill
To empty a sail of wind, so as to make it ineffective, or to lessen the strain on the sail.

Spinnaker
A large balloon-shaped sail used when running before the wind.

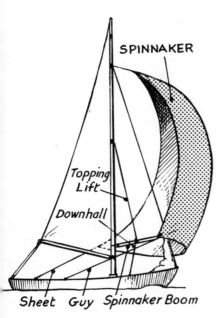

SPINNAKER

Topping Lift

Downhall

Sheet   Guy   Spinnaker Boom

Spit
A small projection of land running into the sea; a long underwater shoal.

Spitfire
A small jib, often made of canvas, used in very rough weather.

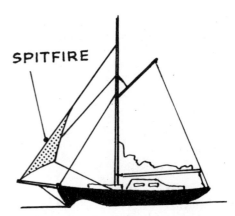

SPITFIRE

Splicing
Joining the ends of a rope or ropes, done by intertwining the strands, as with two pieces to increase the length, or of one piece returning on itself to form a loop.

A

B

Shortsplice

Longsplice

131

Spline Deck

A deck in which thin strips of wood are wedged and glued into seams between planking.

Spreaders

Metal or wood on struts placed athwart a ship's mast in order to spread the angle of the upper shrouds. Called cross trees in older rigs.

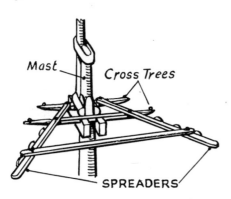

Springs

Mooring lines that lead aft from the bow and forward from the stern (fore spring and back spring respectively) and which prevent the ship surging forwards and backwards alongside the quay. When leaving the quay hauling on one or the other of them swings the bow or stern out as required.

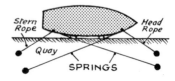

Spring Tides

The high tides that occur twice every month, one or two days before and after new and full moon, when sun, earth, and moon are in line either in conjunction or opposition.

Sprit

A spar, with the sail named after it, reaching diagonally from a mast to the upper outer corner of a sail, to raise and stretch it. The spritsail was used particularly on Thames barges.

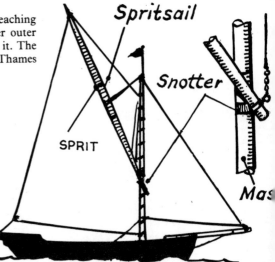

punyarn

rope made by twisting together two- or
three-rope yarns, used for servings and small
lashings.

---

squall

A sudden gust of wind, as in a thunderstorm, a violent wind of brief duration.
There are black and white squalls, black
squalls are attended with black and heavy
clouds, white squalls come unexpectedly
without cloud warning. A common occurrence and a threat to one's safety in small
sailing boats. What may happen is shown in
the sketch.

A is sailing on starboard tack and is likely
to capsize.

B is running with the wind to port. She
may gybe and may swamp.

C is running with the boom to starboard
and may escape with a torn sail.

D is on starboard tack; her sail may swing
across and may damage heads or gear,
and possibly capsize.

E is free on the starboard tack, her sail will
shake and should escape serious damage.

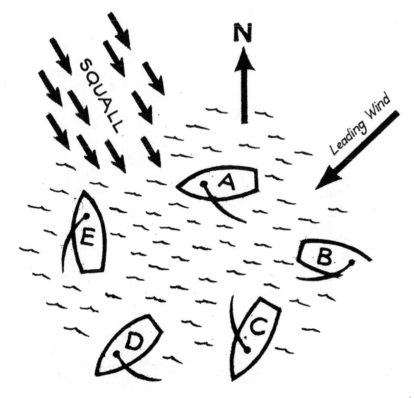

Square Rig

Square-rigged applies to any vessel having the principal sails extended by horizontal cross-yards slung at the middle from the mast instead of by booms, gaffs, stays, etc.

Stability

The equilibrium of a vessel so placed that if disturbed it returns to its former position, as in the case when the centre of gravity is below the point or axis of support.

Stanchions

Upright posts of timber or iron that carry guard lines round the gunwale of a vessel.

Standing Rigging

The ropes which sustain the masts and remain fixed in their position, as the shrouds and stays. Sometimes they are adjustable.

Starboard

The right-hand side of a vessel facing forward.

Starboard Tack

Sailing with the wind on the starboard side of the sails.

GOOD STABILITY   Top heavy

Centre of weight too high

Centre of weight low

Bottom heavy   BAD STABILITY

Station Pointer

A three-armed projector for locating on a chart the position of a vessel from which the angles subtended by three distant objects, whose positions are known, have been observed.

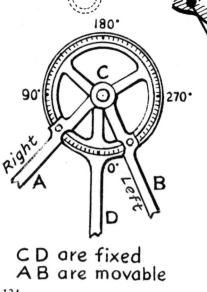

CD are fixed
AB are movable

Station Pointer
holding arms from you.

Stave
To smash a hole in something, ie, a ship's side.

Stay in
1) Part of standing rigging which supports a mast in the fore-and-aft line, hence; forestay and backstay. (2) Refers to situation of ship in relation to anchor and cable. The cable is at 'short stay' when taut and steep with shallow catenary.

Stayband
A metal loop round the mast with eyes to take the stays.

Stays
The moment in going about when a sailing vessel is head to wind. If she fails in this operation she is said to be 'in stays'.

Stealer
In boatbuilding, a short insert of planking at ends worked in among other strakes, that fall short of the required length.

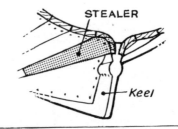

Steaming Box
For the construction of a small boat, a simple arrangement for bending timber for ribbing, or planking, by using a length of rainwater piping, a rubber connection, boiler, and heater.

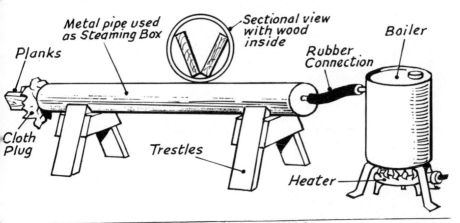

Staysail
A triangular sail, also called the fore-staysail, is usually the sail immediately forward of the mast. The sail can be set from various stays.

Steady
A helm order to keep the direction of the vessel's head on course, or unchanged.

Steaming Lights
The white masthead lights that must be carried by vessels under power as laid down in the 'Rules of the Road'. They must show from dead ahead to two points abaft either beam.

Steerage
The affect of the helm on the vessel. *Steerage way*, means sufficient movement of a vessel to enable it to be controlled by the helm.

Stem

(1) A curved piece of timber to which the two sides of a boat are united at the fore end. (2) To make way against the tide.

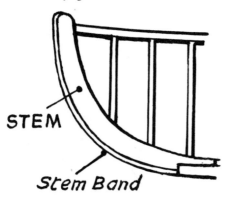

Stemson

A piece of curved timber giving additional support to the stem, keelson, and apron in a vessel's frame near the bow.

Step

(1) A block of wood with a·hole in it, or a solid platform upon the keelson, supporting the heel of a mast. (2) To place the mast in position.

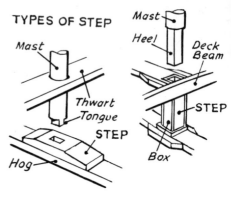

Stern

The after or rear end of a vessel, or of a boat.

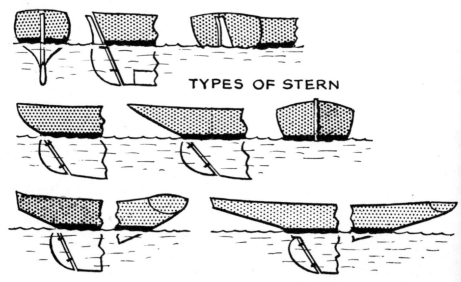

Sternboard
The backward motion of a vessel when going astern, owing to wind or tide. The expression is, 'to make a sternboard'.

Stern-post
The vertical post at the stern of a vessel to which the rudder is secured.

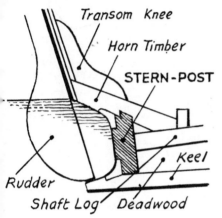

Sternway
The deliberate motion astern of a vessel. Strictly speaking, only power boats make sternway. Under sail, vessels carried astern by current or wind make sternboard; but the differentiation is not kept rigidly.

Stiff
Said of a sailing vessel that does not heel easily under press of sail.

Stock
The horizontal cross-piece of the traditional fisherman anchor set at right angles to the plane of the flukes.

Stocks
The timbers on which a vessel rests during construction, forming an inclined plane from which it may be slid into the water.

Stopper
A short length of rope used to take the strain on a large rope or hawser that is too great to be held by the hand, by 'passing a stopper' to take the weight while the rope is being belayed.

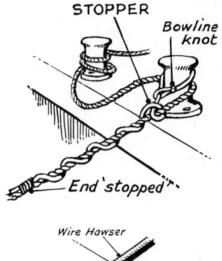

Stopper Knot
The term applied to such knots as the Turk's head or the Mathew Walker which form a knob in the end of a rope to stop it running out through an eye, ringbolt, or dead-eye. A figure-of-eight knot is also used in this way especially to prevent the ends of sheets running out through blocks or fairlead.

137

Stops

Bindings of weak yarn called 'stopping twine' used to secure temporarily a furled sail. 'Setting a jib up in stops' is to furl it up along its luff and secure it in this way and then to hoist it. A sharp tug on the sheets will 'break the sail out' when you need it.

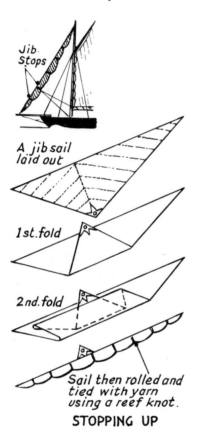

Jib Stops

A jib sail laid out

1st. fold

2nd. fold

Sail then rolled and tied with yarn using a reef knot.

STOPPING UP

Storm Cone

A black cone, hoisted by shore stations as a storm signal; if the point is upwards, the storm is expected from the north, if downwards, from the south.

Strakes

Planks or plates forming continuous lines on the bottom and sides of a vessel, reaching from the stem to the stern. The various strakes are named according to their position, as, for instance—the 'garboard strakes' which are next to the keel followed by the 'bilge strakes', the 'wales', then the upper parts of the sides, the 'sheer strakes'.

Strand

One of the principal twists or parts of a rope, consisting of fibres, yarns, or wires twisted together. Three strands form a rope, though more may be employed.

Stretchers

Narrow cross-pieces in the bottom of a pulling boat against which a rower presses his feet when pulling on the oars.

Strike

To lower down, ie, to strike the topmast.

Stringers

Fore-and-aft members extending from stem to stern inside framing on ribs and fastened thereto, to assist in bracing the ribs.

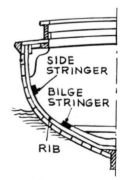

SIDE STRINGER

BILGE STRINGER

RIB

Stopwaters

Soft wooden plugs, or other material inserted at the points where the rabbet line cuts the joins in stem, keel, or deadwood, to render them watertight.

Strop

A ring of rope fitted round a spar or block, or used as a sling for hoisting.

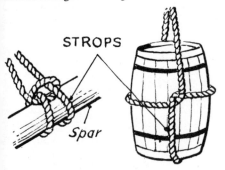

STROPS

Spar

Studding Sail

(pronounced '*stuns'l*'). A light sail set at the side of a principal or square sail of a vessel in free winds to increase her speed. Its head is bent to a small spar which is called the 'studding sail' boom.

Surge

(1) To pay out and check a line or hawser which is turned several times round a capstan or winch. This enables you to slack off gradually and under control. (2) The scend or run of the sea into a harbour.

Swallow

The space between the two shells of a block in which the sheave is fitted.

Sweat

To tighten up a halyard by taking a turn under the cleat and taking up the slack after hauling horizontally on the standing post. Also referred to as 'swigging'.

Sweep

A long heavy oar.

Swell

The large waves resulting from storms and high winds. It spreads outward from the storm centre and can be felt thousands of miles away.

Swing

To steady a ship on a number of known bearings or transits so that compensatory adjustments can be made in order to minimize compass deviation.

T

Tabernacle

A boxlike step for a hinged mast with the after side open, so that the mast can be lowered to pass under bridges, etc.

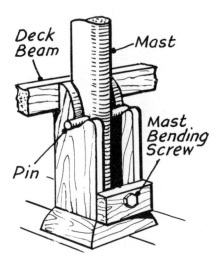

Deck Beam — Mast

Mast Bending Screw

Pin

Tabling

The broad hem or reinforcing strip on the leech or foot of a sail, to receive the boltrope.

Tachometer

An important instrument for showing the speed of a revolving shaft, consisting of a delicate revolving conical pendulum which is driven by the shaft. The action of the pendulum, by change of speed, moves a pointer which indicates the speed on a graduated dial.

Tack

(1) The lower fore corner of a sail. (2) To change the course of a sailing-boat so as to bring the wind round, by the head, to the other side of the boat. (3) The direction in which a boat sails, considered in relation to the position of her sails; also, the distance of the course run at one time in such direction.

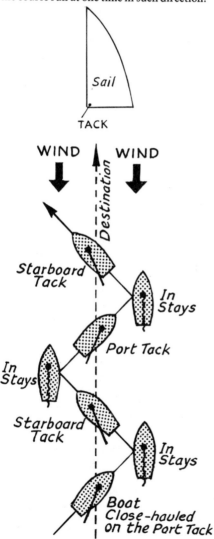

Tackle

(pronounced '*taikle*'). A purchase formed by a rope rove through one or more blocks, of which there are a number of combinations. The amount of power gained differs with each tackle.

Tack Tackle

A small double whiptackle, used for hauling down the tack of a sail.

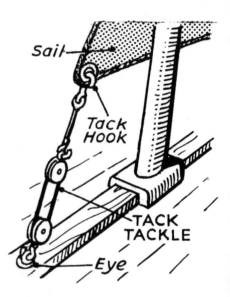

Taffrail

The rail around the stern of a ship.

Tail

(1) A block having a line attached to connect it to an object. (2) A rope tail is sometimes attached to a wire halyard. (3) The end of a line round a winch for hauling on.

Take

(1) *Take in*, to lower or gather in, or furl a sail. (2) *Take up*; said of a boat's planking when it swells and becomes watertight.

ang

he metal fitting formed by thicknesses of ates hung on a through bolt, to which rouds and stays are secured to the mast.

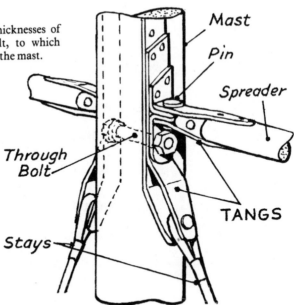

elltale

1) Traditionally a small compass attached o the deckhead in the master's cabin so that e could check the ship's course while lying n his bunk! (2) Short lengths of wool tied to ne shrouds which enable the inexperienced elmsman to see the wind.

ender

(1) Said of a sailing vessel that heels easily nder press of sail. (2) A small dinghy or aunch used to fetch and carry from parent essel.

enon

he tongue on the end of a mast, made to fit to the step.

himble

round metal ring, grooved, so as to fit ithin an eye-splice, to protect it from chaf-g.

horough Foot

) A disarranged condition of a tackle aused by one or both blocks getting turned ver and twisting the ropes. (2) Taking the vist out of a rope by coiling it down in a gure-of-eight.

Throat

The upper fore corner of a boom-and-gaff sail, or of a staysail; that end of a gaff which is next to the mast.

Thwarts

Seats placed across a boat, upon which the oarsman or crewmen sit.

Tidal Streams

The movement of water caused by the *tidal wave*, which in turn produces tidal streams in and out of harbours and along the coast.

Tide

The rise and fall of ocean waters due to the attraction of moon and sun. The tide ebbs and flows twice in each lunar day, or the space of a little more than twenty-four hours.

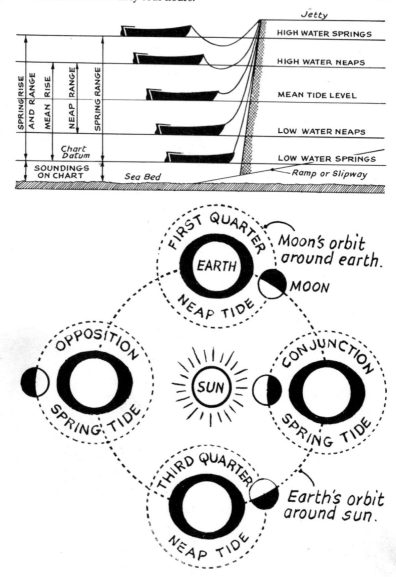

RANGE AND RISE OF THE TIDES

Tide Rode
When a vessel, at anchor, swings by the force of the tide. *Tide way* is mid-stream where the tide runs strongest.

Tight
Free from leaks.

Tiller
A wood or metal bar fitted to head of rudder for steering. Also, the 'tiller' ropes connected to the steering.

Timbers
Frames or 'ribs' curving up on either side at intervals along the whole length of the boat; held in position inside the boat by long fore-and-aft strips of wood called *stringers*. They are covered with planking.

Timing
A special watch used in yacht and boat racing, and other competitions. A time-keeper's stop-watch, it has to be synchronized with the official starter's clock before a race can begin.

Tingle
A temporary patch placed over a broken plank or hole. It is either of metal or wood and nailed with a piece of tarred canvas in between the patch and hole.

Toe Straps
Toe-holds used when leaning outboard to balance a sailing dinghy.

Toggle
A wooden pin tapering toward both ends with a groove around its middle, to insert in the bight or loop of a rope, often used with a 'becket'. Also useful for temporarily holding a tiller, or holding a sail cover over a boom, etc.

Top Hamper
The necessary minimum weight carried aloft, such as, rigging, spars, lights, etc, of a vessel.

Topping Lift
A part of the running rigging employed to raise or top the outer end of a boom. Its main function is to keep the boom off the deck when the mainsail is not hoisted.

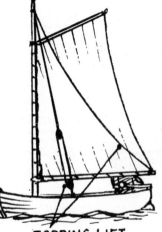

TOPPING LIFT

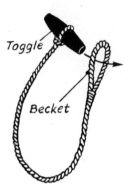

Toggle

Becket

143

Towing

No standard method of towing, or being taken in tow can be laid down because of the types of vessels involved. To be considered is the condition of the towed vessel, the distance of tow, weather, and other factors. The length of tow-line is most important, the longer it is the more even the tension will be during the time of towing, thus easing the strain of slackening and tightening. Sketch shows a dinghy being towed astern.

Some tips are: if the towing boat is to maintain its manoeuvrability, the tow rope must be made fast forward—not at the stern; the towing boat goes to windward of the boat being picked up so as to be able to throw it a line; the tow rope can be 'damped down' (to help to eliminate sharp jerks) by inserting a medium-sized tyre or attaching a heavy weight near the middle of the rope.

A towing method reducing drag by using the side of the wave in the wake of the towing vessel.

Tracks and Slides

Fittings attached to the mast to allow the sail to be hauled up or down; used in lieu of hoops or parrel bands.

The track is of course screwed on to the mast and the slides attached to the eyelets in the luff with webbing or strong nylon thread. Plastic slides have virtually replaced metal ones owing to the expense of the latter although metal slides are generally thought to run more smoothly. The slides can be fastened directly on to the eyelets but the use of a thimble lessens chafe and should always be employed except in an emergency.

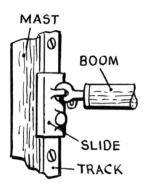

Trade Winds

Tropical winds blowing towards the equator from 30° North and 30° South. The doldrums being on the equator where sailing vessels are often becalmed, owing to lack of wind.

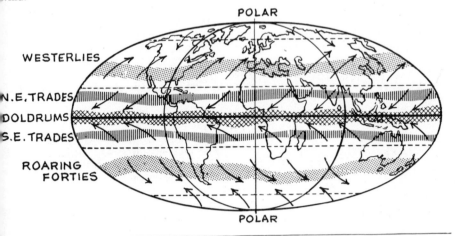

POLAR

WESTERLIES

N.E. TRADES
DOLDRUMS
S.E. TRADES

ROARING FORTIES

POLAR

Transom

A broad transverse area, either flat or slightly curved at the after end of a vessel.

Trapeze Harness

A harness devised for racing dinghies and used over recent years to enable a crewman to use his weight to greater advantage, by balancing his weight overboard when laying up to windward.

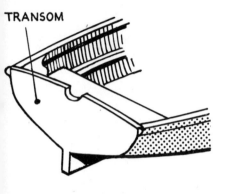

TRANSOM

145

Traveller

An iron ring which moves along a rope, spar, or boom, etc; eg, the bowsprit traveller which carries the tack of the jib to the end of the bowsprit.

Traverse Sailing

A sailing by compound courses; the method or process of finding the resulting course and distance from a series of different shorter courses and distances actually passed *over* by a vessel. To *work* or solve a traverse is to reduce a series of courses and distances to a single one, by the use of a Traverse Table.

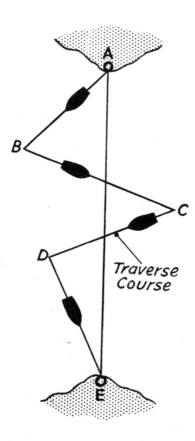

Traverse Course

Traverse Tables

Navigation tables which contain the true difference of latitude and departure corresponding to every course from 0° to 90° and for every distance from 1 nautical mile to 300 miles. See also *Departure*.

Treenails

(pronounced '*tren'ls*'). Hardwood pegs used as ship fastening.

Triatic Stay

A stay running from the mainmast to the foremast head in a schooner.

Trice

To draw up the tack of a sail by means of a rope rove through a block at the hounds or the gaffjaws so as to let the wind out of a sail without lowering it.

Trim

(1) To adjust sails, so as to present the most favourable angle to the wind. (2) A smart appearance. (3) To balance a fore-and-aft vessel on the water by adjustment of weight.

Trimaran

A three-hulled yacht, the two smaller hulls are joined to the centre hull with cross-arms. These craft are known for their stability.

Tripping Line

A light line buoyed at one end and attached to the crown of an anchor at the other; used to free the anchor from any obstruction by capsizing or 'tripping' it. Also a temporary line rove under the sheave in the heel of a topmast for hoisting or lowering it.

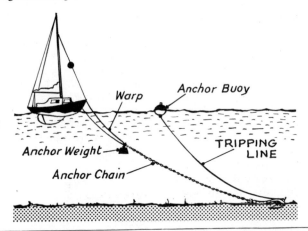

Tropics

The two parallels of latitude 23°27' north and south of the equator (Cancer and Capricorn respectively) where the sun is directly overhead during the summer solstices in the northern and southern hemispheres.

Trot

Of moorings; a long, single ground chain to which numerous individual rising chains are attached giving a long line of small-boat moorings in a comparatively small space. Also used to describe a number of small vessels moored alongside each other.

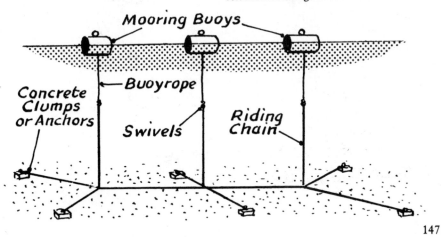

Truck

A circular piece of wood fitted to the mast-head, to protect the end-grain and to carry sheaves for the flag halyards.

True Course

Is the angle 'AOS' that the vessel's track makes with the true, or geographical, meridian, indicating true north and south.

Truss

An iron ring or looped rope securing the centre of a yard to a mast, by which it swings.

Trysail

A triangular sail of strong canvas with a short luff and long foot, hoist on a yacht's mainmast when the wind is too strong even for a deep-reefed mainsail. Set in conjunction with the storm jib it permits the vessel to make to windward even under extreme conditions—a vital requirement if caught on a lee shore.

Tufnol

A laminated plastic material widely used in making blocks. These are strong and lighter than the wooden blocks, do not rot, and are lubricated by water.

Tumble-Home

The inward curve of the topsides.

Tunnel-Hull-Boat

A boat similar to a catamaran, but designed to make full use of aerodynamic forces in high-speed racing. The narrow planing surfaces of the two hulls allow the boat to plane only on the after-part when at great speed. It is the tunnel between the two hulls with an unrestricted exit which produces the aerodynamic lift.

Turk's Head

An ornamental stopper knot resembling a turban.

Turn

To pass a rope once or twice round a cleat or bollard, in order to secure it.

Turnbuckle

See *Bottle Screw*.

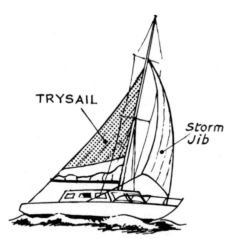

TRYSAIL

Storm Jib

rning

motor-boat swings round from the stern,
d sharp turns are not possible at full speed.
erefore, speed must be reduced. To turn in
estricted space, turn the wheel hard over
en rev up again. This enables the boat to
rn in little more than its own length. Wher-
er possible turns should be made in the
ection of the rotational throw of the pro-
ller, which will give better manoeuvrabi-
y.

Track of pivoting point of boat

* The stern requires more attention than the bow when manoeuvring. It is the stern which moves in response to the rudder, and not the bow, this is important

---

J

na Rig

small float rig consisting of a large gaff or
gsail main and no headsails.

nbend

o cast loose or untie a rope.

nderfoot

) Under a vessel's bottom. (2) A term used
hen an anchor is lowered and carried short
f the bottom, especially when a first anchor
dragging.

nder-Run

cable passed over the bows and stern of the
oat, while men haul the boat along by pul-
ng along the cable.

Under the Lee (of)
Under the shelter of land or an object.

Undertow
The current that sets seaward near the
bottom when waves are breaking upon the
shore.

Under Way
Having free movement through the water.

'Upside Down' Building
A method of building which eliminates the
use of stocks. A plan is made and then trans-
ferred, full size, to the floor, where the exact
position of each frame can be marked out
ready for assembling.

149

V

Vane

Used on shipboard as a weathercock. (1) Any plate or arm, or similar device, attached to an axis and exposed to a moving current, as of air. (2) A small length of bunting used as a wind indicator, is often called a dog vane.

Vangs

Ropes controlling the lateral movement of the afterend of a gaff or a sprit. In the USA and the antipodes the term is used for the kicking strap which holds the boom down when running.

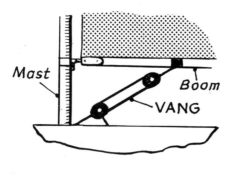

Variation

Is the angle between *true* North and *magnetic* North; it varies in different parts of the world, and may be either easterly or westerly. Variation may increase or decrease from year to year, so the magnetic bearing may also change. Therefore, when plotting a compass course make sure your chart is up-to-date.

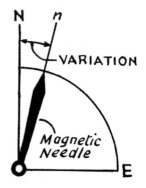

Veer

(1) The wind is said to *veer*, if the point from which it blows shifts in a clockwise direction, and *back*, if it shifts in the opposite direction. (2) To pay out a ship's anchor cable.

Ventilation

The free flow of fresh air below decks is essential to counteract dry rot, ill-health, and the accumulation of petrol and gas fumes.

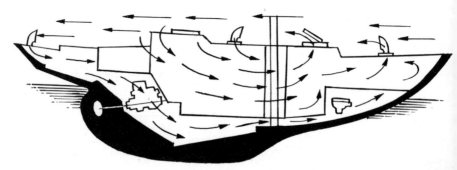

Ventilator

A coaming secured to the deck through which air circulates to various compartments. There are many types and sizes of ventilators now on the market. Some ventilators are not suitable for offshore boats as water can enter them when the boat heels over.

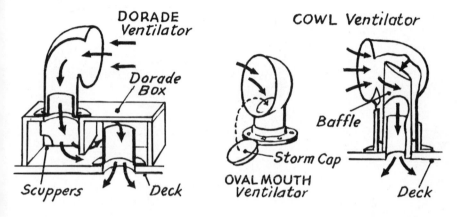

DORADE Ventilator

Dorade Box

Scuppers   Deck

COWL Ventilator

Baffle

Storm Cap

OVAL MOUTH Ventilator

Deck

Vernier

A sliding scale, invented by Pierre Vernier, a French mathematician, for obtaining fractional parts of the sub-divisions of a sextant, or barometer.

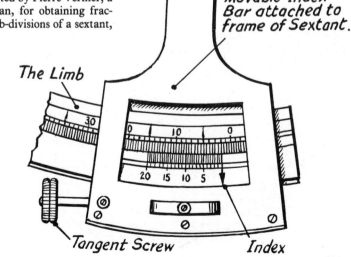

The Limb

Movable Index Bar attached to frame of Sextant.

Tangent Screw   Index

Vertical Danger Angle

An offshore distance measured by the vertical angle subtended by an object of known height. Used when passing a submerged danger such as a rock. For example ½ mile (800m) clearance is required of a rock to seaward of a landmark known to be 200ft (61m) high above sea level. AD is 200ft (61m) DC is 1 mile (1.6km), so in order to keep DC equal to 1 mile (1.6km) you must keep the angle ACD constant by using a sextant.

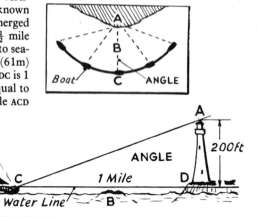

W

Wale

The outer wale, or strake of a boat which runs beneath and supports the outer edge of the gunwale. 'Wales' are also, strong, strengthening planks in a vessel's sides, running her entire length fore and aft, just above the water-line.

Wall-Knot

A knot made by unlaying the strands of a rope, and passing them among each other to prevent their untwisting. Also used as a stopper knot or collar.

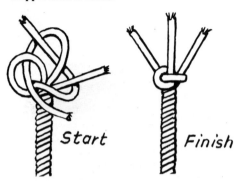

Warp

(1) A rope used in hauling or moving a vessel or boat, usually with one end attached to an anchor, a post, or other fixed object; a towing-line. (2) Of timber; to twist and lose shape. (3) The lengthwise measurement and thread of cloth.

Watch

(1) Division of a ship's company apportioned to various duties in rota.

(2) *Using your watch as a compass.* To find your bearings in day time with the aid of a watch, point the figure twelve on the face of your watch at the sun, then draw a line from the centre of the watch to a point midway between the hour hand and the figure twelve when the line will be pointing, in the Southern Hemisphere, North, and in the Northern Hemisphere, South.

Water-Line

(1) The line to which water rises. (2) One of the lines bounding horizontal sections of a vessel's hull, and corresponding with the water-level at various loads; as, the *light* water-line or the *load* water-line.

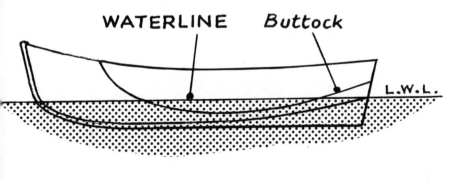

Water Movement

Sailing down a coast can be hazardous to all craft at any time. Therefore, a careful study should be made of the look of the water and its movement.

Rocks Waves with ragged, breaking crests give warning of rocks just below the surface.

Shoal A place where water is not deep, indicated by a shine on the water suggesting a sandbank.

Reef A chain of rocks lying submerged near the surface.

Tide-rip Is indicated by a rippling of the surface; often caused by an overfall—a wave that breaks sharply; at the meeting of conflicting currents, or a rise in the sea bed.

Trochoidal (Wheel-like motion). Open-sea waves of a swell, often left-over from a passing storm, not usually dangerous.

Cycloidal (A circle rolling along a straight line). A wind-driven wave, the stronger the wind the larger the wave, depending on the fetch (distance) the wave travels; can be dangerous.

Slick A smooth place on a surface of water, caused by a fast tide.

Channel The deepest part of a passage through which a tidal stream runs, often marked by buoys.

Overfalls Turbulent stretch of sea, etc, caused by waves breaking sharply over shoals or by meeting of currents.

Bar A shallow bank usually of silt or sand across the mouth of a river or estuary. With an ebb-tide and a strong onshore wind the seas will break dangerously over it.

Waves

Waves are caused by the increasing force of the wind on the surface of the sea. The wave travels along the surface of the sea before the wind, the water itself merely rising and falling as the wave passes. A swell is a much

153

larger wave caused by a wind at a distance, or a recent wind. A wave is formed by the movement of water particles revolving at and below the surface, which gives a wave its shape.

Direction of wave caused by the wind. ➡

Revolving water particles

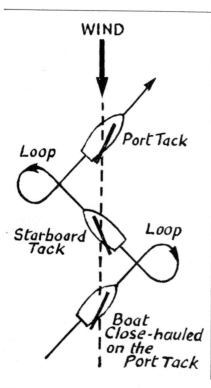

WIND

Loop

Port Tack

Starboard Tack

Loop

Boat Close-hauled on the Port Tack

Ways
(1) The timbers on which a vessel is launched. (2) To be in motion, as, when a vessel starts to move. *Headway*, making forward movement, *sternway*, making progress astern, *leeway*, progressing to leeward.

Wear
To change tack by gybing the ship round before the wind. A manoeuvre used by square-riggers which sometimes had difficulty in going about.

Weather
(1) Windward, ie, weather side. (2) To pass safely to windward of a danger.

Weather Helm
A tendency on the part of a sailing vessel to come up in the wind, rendering it necessary to keep the tiller to windward to counteract it.

Weather-Map

The Meteorological Department publishes daily a weather-map showing weather conditions over a wide area. The map may look complicated but is not difficult to follow. From this, one can learn the general pattern of the warm and cold fronts and the distribution of high- and low-pressure areas. With the aid of an aneroid barometer, in conjunction with press and radio reports, a yachtsman should feel able to forecast the weather he will meet. *Meteorological Symbols* are also shown in the diagram.

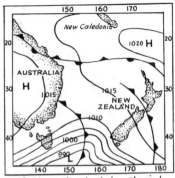

In the northern hemisphere the wind blows clockwise around the centre of high pressures.

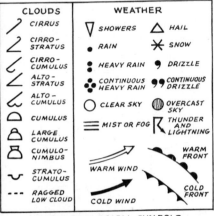

METEOROLOGICAL SYMBOLS

Weather-Ship

A ship maintained to monitor weather conditions in mid-ocean.

Balloon carrying radar reflector by which direction of wind may be watched on radar screen.

Weather-Tide

A tide which sets against the lee side of a vessel, impelling her to the windward.

Weft

The width measurement and thread from selvage to selvage in a sail cloth.

Weigh

To raise the anchor from the sea-bed.

Well

(1) The cockpit. (2) The lower part of a ship's bilges.

Wend

Synonym for 'to tack'. Not often used.

Wheel

The wheel and axle mechanism used, instead of a tiller, for steering.

Wheelhouse

The shelter containing the helmsman, the wheel, steering compass, and the helm indicator.

155

Whip

A small hoisting tackle with one block and a single rope, used to hoist light loads. A *double* whip has double the pulling power—that is, weight of one unit on the hauling part will balance a weight of two units on the movable hook block.

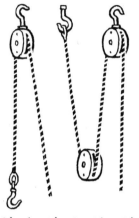

Single Whip Double Whip

Whipping

The end of a rope bound with spunyarn to prevent fraying. The two main methods of whipping are the *common whipping* which is done by hand, or the *palm and needle whipping* which is more permanent.

Whisker Pole

A pole with jaws on one end and a spike on the other, extending outwards on either side of the mast to hold the jib out when running 'goosewinged'.

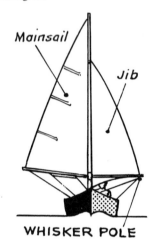

Mainsail

Jib

WHISKER POLE

Whiskers

Bowsprit 'spreaders'.

Winch

In ships and large vessels winches are operated by steam or electric motors. For smaller craft a hand-winch may be fitted on the deck to lighten the task of hauling in the anchor, tightening sheets, or hauling a boat onto a trailer.

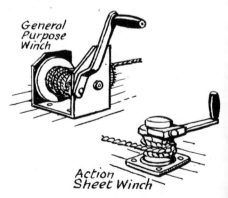

General Purpose Winch

Action Sheet Winch

ind

ae wind is just air in motion, and it moves
cause pressure in one place is higher than
other. As a general rule, the force of the
rface wind on land is three-fifths that of
e wind at sea. In sailing there are two kinds
winds, *true* and *apparent*. The first is the
tual wind felt when the vessel is stationary.
ae second is an apparent distortion of the
st caused by the vessel's forward motion.
ne indicators in the diagram do, of course,
ow the apparent wind.

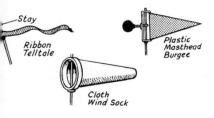

Stay
Ribbon
Telltale
Plastic
Masthead
Burgee
Cloth
Wind Sock

indlass

wheel and axle mechanism used for hau-
ıg in chain, cable, etc.

ind Rode

aid of a moored vessel that swings to the
ınd rather than the tide, cf, *tide rode*.

indsail

anvas funnel used to deflect cool air below
cks in hot weather.

indward

he point or side from which the wind blows,
opposed to *leeward*.

ing and Wing

aid of a schooner, or her sails, when going
efore the wind with the foresail on one side
nd the mainsail on the other, cf, *goose-
inged*.

iring

he stringer upon which the thwarts rest in
nall boats.

Wishbone

A divided spar between whose curved arms
the clew of a fore-and-aft sail is extended, the
curvature allowing for the belly of the sail.
Can only be used in two-masted vessels such
as ketch and schooner.

Work

(1) A word applied to a vessel when her
planking and timbers are under strain in a
heavy sea and letting water in. (2) To manoeuvre a vessel.

Worm

To wind a rope, yarn, or other material spirally round, in the lay of a cable, etc.

Wring

To subject anything to unfair twisting strain
or torque.

Y

Yacht

A vessel specially built for racing, or cruising
for pleasure; either sail- or power-driven.

Yankee

A high-cut jib topsail, mostly used in yacht-
racing. Often seen in the modern cutter and
the masthead cutter.

Yankee
Jib

Yard

A long slender spar, nearly cylindrical but tapering from the middle part towards the ends, suspended crosswise on a mast and used to support sails; they are called *square* when the yard hangs parallel with the deck, and *lateen* when it hangs obliquely. Also used for hoisting flags.

Yawl

A two-masted sailing vessel rigged fore an aft with the mizzen mast stepped aft of th rudder head. The advantage of this rig (a with ketch) is that it can be sailed without th mainsail at all in a strong wind.

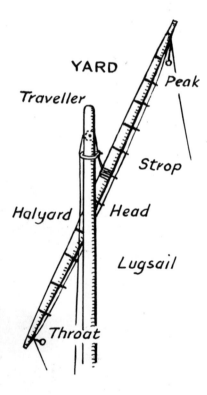

Yarn

A kind of fibrous, spun thread used for rope-making.

Yaw

To swing from side to side of the desired course usually the result of a strong following wind and sea but often evidence of bad helmsmanship.

Yoke

A cross-piece fitted to the rudder head t which lines are attached by which the boat i steered.

Zenith

The point in the heavens immediately above the observer.

Zenith Distance

The angle between the observer's zenith and a observed celestial body subtended at the earth's centre.

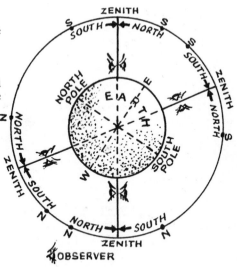

Zones

The five great regions of the earth, with respect to latitude and temperature. The *torrid* zone, extending from tropic to tropic 26°56'; or 23°28' on each side of the equator; two *temperate* or *variable* zones, situated between the tropics and the polar circles; and two *frigid* zones, situated between the polar circles and the poles.

Zone Times

The division of the world by meridians of longitude into zones or sectors where the same time is kept.

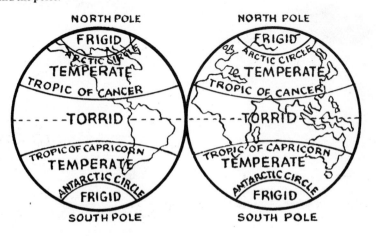

GLOSSARY OF NAUTICAL TERMS

Before handling a boat, any aspiring sailor should first learn the correct sea terms when hand
ling ropes or boats. These were designed for a purpose and should be adhered to.

Avast	Stop lowering. Hold fast.
Avast hauling	An order to stop.
Back up	To haul taut on the free end of a rope which is round a bollard o post.
Belay	To secure a rope round some fixture, such as a cleat or bollard.
Bowse (down)	To pull down on a rope in order to 'harden up' on it.
Cast off	To let go and free a rope which is belayed or made fast.
Check	To ease out on a rope or sheet under control.
Hand	(1) A term used for one of the crew. (2) *To hand*: to lower a sail an stow it.
Handsomely	Slowly, with care, eg, lower handsomely.
Harden up	To tighten up on a rope or sheet.
Haul away	An order to haul steady.
Heave	(1) To lift or give a strong pull together. (2) *To heave*, or to pull o throw a rope.
Hoist	To haul on a rope when a weight is to be lifted.
Hoist away	An order to hoist steadily until further orders.
Let draw	To allow a sail to fill on a desired tack.
Let fly	To let go the sheets completely.
Let go	Of an anchor, to let it drop into the water.
Light to	To fleet a rope back along the deck to enough slack to belay it.
Lower away	To lower steadily.
Make fast	Securing a rope so that it will hold fast when the strain comes on it.
Roundly	Quickly, smartly.
Slack away	To pay out a rope by hand without losing control of it.
Snub	To restrain suddenly a rope that is being checked.
Take a turn	To pass a rope around some fixture one or more times to take th strain so long as the end is held.
To haul	To pull on a rope *by hand*.
To haul taut	To take the strain.
Well enough	Stop hauling or checking.
Walk back	To haul on a rope by walking back with rope in hand.